Records Management

RECORDS MANAGEMENT

A Practical Guide

Susan Z. Diamond

amacom

AMERICAN MANAGEMENT ASSOCIATIONS

Library of Congress Cataloging in Publication Data

Diamond, Susan Z.
    Records management,

    Bibliography: p.
    Includes index.
    1. Records—Management. I. American Management
Associations. II. Title.
HF5736.D48   1983   651.5   82-18477
ISBN 0-8144-5729-0

First Printing

To my mother,
Henrietta Wood Diamond,
with love and admiration

Foreword

This book provides a comprehensive source of information on all aspects of records management. And if your records management program is to be a success, it must eventually encompass all of these areas. The challenge is intensified by the changes data processing and office automation have brought to records management. Consequently, this book integrates the fundamentals of records management—which have not lost their validity—with automated methods for processing and handling information.

The ideas in this book have been tested repeatedly through my consulting practice and communicated to hundreds of participants in American Management Associations seminars. I am grateful to all of the individuals I've worked with for the interchange of ideas, as well as for the continued enthusiasm and support for this book.

Thanks are also due to the AMACOM staff, in particular my editor, Rob Kaplan. He did a superb job with my first book, *Preparing Administrative Manuals,* and has been equally helpful with this one.

Of course, no foreword is complete without an expression of gratitude to one's spouse. But in my case, an omission would be unpardonable. Allan has supported me in this effort, just as he has in every venture I've undertaken. We are a team, and this book is his as well as mine.

Susan Z. Diamond

Contents

CHAPTER 1

The Role of Records Management

Records management is still a relatively new concept. A 1976 survey of members of the Association of Records Managers and Administrators, Inc. revealed that most of the companies surveyed originated their records management programs after 1950. Because records management is a comparatively young discipline, top management is often ill-informed about the need for records management and the benefits it provides. A common misconception is that records management is simply a fancy name for the storage and destruction of inactive records. Another misconception is that the term "records" refers only to hard copy (paper) documents.

DEFINITIONS

To clarify matters, let's review some key definitions. A "record" is "any form of recorded information." The means of recording the information may be paper, film (usually microfilm), or any magnetic medium such as computer tapes or disks. In other words, practically any information created or communicated within the organization, except unrecorded conversations, forms a record.

Records typically have a four-stage life cycle. First, there is creation, when pen is put to paper, data is generated by a computer, or information is captured on film, tape, or any other medium. Next is the period of active use, which can range from a few days to several years. During this period, users frequently reference the record and need quick access to it. Consequently, the record is maintained in the office area. Most records have an active life of one to two years.

The third period in the cycle is when the record is inactive and in storage. During this period, the record is kept either because of legal reasons or because of users' infrequent reference needs. To reduce costs, the record is stored in a special nonoffice area known as a records center. Some records may have no inactive period, while others may remain in this stage for several years or even "permanently" (that is, for the life of the organization).

The final stage in the cycle is destruction, which occurs when the organization no longer needs the record and is no longer required by law to keep it. With confidential or proprietary records, special precautions must be taken to insure that destruction is total and the records can in no way be recreated.

As I've already mentioned, a common misconception is that records management involves only the latter two stages of a record's life. In reality, records management is concerned with controlling records from their creation, through both active and inactive periods, to their destruction. When properly implemented, this total concept means preventing the creation of unnecessary records and unnecessary extra copies; insuring the efficient, economical use of records in both the active and inactive periods; and destroying records as soon as they're not needed. Thus, records management has the dual goals of promoting the efficient retrieval and use of information and keeping records maintenance costs to a minimum. These goals are not mutually exclusive, as you'll see throughout this book.

RECORDS MANAGEMENT IS . . .

With the comprehensive definition I've just outlined, records management becomes a broad-based discipline, composed of the following areas:

Forms management (the proper design and use of forms—one way of controlling records from their creation).
Reports management (controlling reports in the same way forms management controls forms).
Filing systems (in particular, the management of active records).
Records retention (a system for keeping records as long as necessary, but no longer).

Records center (the storage of inactive records).

Vital records program (the protecting of those records that are essential to the organization's continued existence).

Micrographics (the use of microfilm to increase productivity and conserve space).

Although some organizations' records management programs do not encompass all of these areas, ideally they should all be grouped together to enhance their overall effectiveness. For example, forms management is most effective when it is part of records management, as the overall goals of both programs are quite similar. And if an organization lacks an overall records management program, it will not be able to develop all of these areas logically and consistently.

One area I've not listed that is sometimes included in the records management spectrum is word processing. Word processing deals with the mechanical process of creating records. While records management should take advantage of word processing's capabilities and should govern the organization of information stored by word processing, the two areas are not closely enough linked to merit combination. The same is true of data processing and records management. While there is overlap between the two areas and extensive potential for automating the records management function, neither area is a subgroup of the other.

BENEFITS OF RECORDS MANAGEMENT

Instituting a records management program results in both immediate and long-term benefits to the organization. These benefits include:

Substantial space savings. Implementing a records retention schedule and destroying unnecessary records can reduce the space now occupied by records by 40 percent. The effective use of microfilm also conserves space.

Reducing misfiles. On an average, a misfile costs the organization $80 in clerical time spent searching for the record. Properly designed filing systems reduce the misfile rate substantially.

Faster retrieval of information. Improving filing and storage practices also speeds retrieval.

Reducing filing equipment expenditures. Destroying unneeded records will probably eliminate the need to purchase filing equipment for several years. With the high cost of such equipment, savings can be substantial.

Insuring compliance with legal retention requirements. Organizations without records management run the risk of destroying records too soon and, consequently, not being able to produce them when legally required. Or else they adopt the costly practice of keeping everything forever—a practice that can also backfire in a legal proceeding. The organization is then required to produce everything it has relating to the proceeding, not just what it is legally required to have. At the very least, this producing of all related records is time-consuming and expensive. And depending on the nature of the records, it may jeopardize the organization's case through the admission of unfavorable evidence.

Controlling and reducing the creation of records. Both forms and reports management reduce the amount of records that are created internally.

Protecting the organization's vital records. A disaster can destroy any organization's records. A vital records program insures that the organization has protected copies of those records needed to resume its operations.

The list of benefits provided by a comprehensive records management program is a formidable one. Together these benefits meet our dual goals of increased efficiency and reduced costs and more than justify the cost and effort required to establish a records management program.

CHAPTER 2

Selling the Records Management Concept

In spite of the benefits outlined in Chapter 1, many records managers find their biggest problem is not implementing the program, but convincing others of the need to implement it. The records manager's role as salesperson is further complicated by the fact that two groups must be "sold" on the records management concept: (1) upper management and (2) the main users of the program middle and lower management and their staffs. Each of the two groups has different concerns, and records managers must adapt their sales strategies accordingly.

SELLING THE PROGRAM TO UPPER MANAGEMENT

Before you can successfully sell upper management on the records management concept, you must determine the reasons for its resistance. Usually one or more of the following factors is the root of the problem:

Ignorance of the records management concept. Most upper management personnel are only vaguely aware of what records management involves. They either assume that records management deals only with inactive records or that it is a "fancy" name for filing. Consequently, one of the records manager's first steps must be to "educate" management in this area.

Concern about increased costs. Upper management often feels records management is not "cost-justified." It perceives the program as requiring substantial initial cash outlays with no return on the investment. While records management is not a "profit center," it does save the organization money through the more effective use of existing office space and reduced expenditures for filing equipment. Once management realizes the amount of ongoing expense in these areas, it is much more receptive to records management.

Concern about "empire building." In highly decentralized organizations, there is often a fear that records management will gain too much power or will impede other areas from operating autonomously. Yet the same managers recognize that everyone in the organization must comply with a number of centralized financial procedures. Records management is just one more staff function (like personnel and finance) that crosses departmental lines. And it *must* cross these lines if it is to be effective. A totally decentralized records management program is not records management.

Ignorance of the legal problems that can arise without records management. As legal protection, records management is similar to an insurance policy. You hope you never have to use it, but if you do, you're really glad you have it. When companies are involved in litigation, fast and complete retrieval of relevant records is essential. Also, a consistent records management program helps protect the company from charges of destroying or misplacing records to conceal information. In fact, the records manager may be required to testify about the company's records retention policies and procedures. Because of these factors, many companies belatedly establish records management after litigation occurs—closing the barn door after the horse escapes, although in this case, the saying "better late than never" is true.

Unawareness of the problem. Upper management often doesn't recognize that there is a problem with the company's records. Such symptoms as an office space shortage, rising copier costs, and increased filing equipment expenditures are not linked together. Instead, the symptoms are treated separately through such remedies as open plan offices, new types of filing equipment, and copier controls. While these solutions may be advisable, the first step should be to deal with the real problem—the lack of records management.

SHAPING A STRATEGY

After you've determined why management at *your* company has not established a records management program, you can develop

an appropriate sales strategy. For example, if management ignorance is a problem, you need to address this area first. Many upper
level managers regard records management as a new and untested
discipline rather than a program tried and proved in the past 30
years. One top executive I met with asked, "What is a records
manager and where do you find one? I can't believe these people
exist." Supplying him with a copy of a 1976 survey sponsored by the
Association of Records Managers and Administrators, Inc.
(ARMA) answered the question by explaining what over 800
records managers did, how long their programs had been established, and so on.

Other proven management education tools include taking managers to an ARMA meeting so they can find out firsthand what
other companies are doing; arranging a visit to a company with a
comprehensive, well-run records management program; and giving managers appropriate articles on the subject. Providing rein-
forcement through examples of what other organizations are doing
is important because it defuses any management suspicions of
"empire building," as well as substantiating your recommendations.

As you develop a sales strategy, the most important point to keep
in mind is the needs and concerns of the people you must convince.
For example, if management is concerned with "keeping up with
the Joneses," acquainting it with other companies' programs is a
good starting point. On the other hand, if management is conservative in its approaches or resistant to change, a legal department
presentation about the problems the company can encounter without records management would be helpful. If cost cutting is a
prime concern, document expenditures for filing equipment over
the past five years and the cost of the office space now occupied by
filing equipment. Then point out that implementing records management will make approximately 40 percent of the space available
for other uses and will virtually eliminate purchasing filing equipment for several years.

One last psychological point—don't criticize the company's previous records management practices, if any. The people you are
trying to convince may have established those practices. Instead,
take the approach that the existing system undoubtedly met the
organization's needs initially but is no longer adequate.

SELLING THE PROGRAM IN STAGES

Upper management is unlikely to give you *carte blanche* to implement a full-scale records management program simultaneously throughout the organization—for good reason. Records management is not an area where you should plunge into the deep water and learn to swim as you go. Such an approach virtually guarantees a full-scale disaster. Instead, you should begin with a two-step approach: (1) conducting an initial survey to convince management that a problem exists and (2) selecting a test area for implementing the program.

Conducting an Initial Survey

The initial survey provides the data you'll need to "sell" records management to the corporate decision makers. This survey is not a comprehensive study of the organization's records; that comes later. Instead, it determines what major records problems exist now and helps identify a good test area for the program.

The survey can be handled either through interview/visits to the various departments or through questionnaires followed by interview/visits to key problem areas. With a small organization, you'll probably find interviewing each area simpler and more effective. With a large organization, time constraints will limit you to written questionnaires followed by selective interviews. In either case, you'll be looking for the following information:

Amount of records stored in the department (for now, a count of file drawers will suffice).

Amount of new records added each year (again in file drawers).

Money spent on filing equipment and supplies each year for the past five years.

How many years of records are kept in the office area.

Who handles filing now.

What, if any, filing procedures exist and how they are documented (filing instructions, indexes, and so on).

Problems that have arisen such as the inability to find information, time-consuming searches for misfiled information, filing backlogs, and lack of storage space for records.

This data can be collected quickly with a minimum of effort—an important consideration since, at this stage, you probably have little, if any, funding and few resources for the project.

Selecting a Test Group

You'll use the survey results to select one or two departments for the pilot program. Choose departments that have major problems with their records and that are receptive to participating in the pilot program. The interviews, in particular, will help you determine which departments best meet both qualifications.

Selecting departments with major problems has two advantages. One, it makes sense to attack major problem areas first, as these cost the organization the most in money and resources. These areas can't afford to wait for assistance. Two, using problem areas in the test program gives you the opportunity to achieve dramatic improvements. Once you have a "success story," management will be more receptive to expanding the program to other areas, and other departments will be more eager to participate.

PRESENTING THE PLAN TO MANAGEMENT

After you've collected data on the existing problems and decided on an appropriate test program, you'll need to present your findings to management. The traditional method is a written report summarizing the data and proposing an action plan (which you can develop from the material in subsequent chapters).

However, this report will have more impact if you support it with photographic evidence. One records manager found that photographs of the mildewed boxes and sagging shelves in the company's records center were her best argument for a total overhaul of the center. Photographs of records stored in cardboard boxes in closets and stacked on top of overflowing cabinets in the office area also provide vivid testimony that a problem exists.

In addition to photographs of problem areas, also include illustrations of any new equipment to be purchased and samples of those forms that will be used with the new system. Floor plans showing how much space will be opened up with records management provide further support. Finally, if you can get potential users to comment on the current records problems they face and to support the establishment of a records management program, it will greatly strengthen your case.

If you don't gain immediate approval, don't give up. Instead, analyze management's objections and develop appropriate answers or revise your proposal accordingly. For example, if management feels the initial cost estimate is too high, analyze the proposal to see where costs can be trimmed and what the ultimate effect would be. Perhaps more existing filing equipment could be used instead of replaced, or the new micrographics equipment could be leased initially.

GETTING COOPERATION FROM USERS

Although upper management support is essential for implementing the program, you'll also need strong backing from the program's users. Users can and do "sabotage" management-approved programs when they perceive those programs as being unworthy of their support.

Just as you did with the management group, you'll need to determine the causes for any user resistance to records management. Here the most basic cause is fear—the users' fear of losing control of their records or fear that a critical record will not be found when it's needed. In the comic strip "Peanuts," Linus clings to his security blanket; most users feel the same way about their records. These fears are often coupled with ignorance about the benefits of records management.

Alleviating these fears is a matter of education and user involvement. As an initial step, have each department appoint a *records coordinator*. This individual will serve as a liaison between the records management group and the other members of his or her department. The coordinator should be someone who works well with others and has a good rapport with the rest of the department. The coordinator also should be receptive to new ideas, able to coordinate details well, and a relatively long-term member of the department. While the coordinator can be anyone in the department, an administrative assistant or experienced secretary is often a good choice.

Although all managers will need general information about the records management program, you'll work most closely with the department head and the records coordinator. The department head is responsible for seeing that you get full support for his or her department. To help insure such support, it's a good idea to draft a letter for the signature of the president (or another top executive) that states why the records management program is being implemented and asks everyone involved to give you his or her full support. If you draft the letter, it's much more likely to be sent than if you just ask the executive to write it.

You'll find that your credibility with users increases gradually. If you can substantially help one department, word will spread and other departments will be more receptive. It's especially helpful to identify individuals who are natural leaders and obtain their support for the program. It's also helpful to get the records management program featured in the company newspaper or magazine. Editors of such publications are usually looking for material, and "before and after" photographs are especially effective here. And, of course, a good program is its own best sales tool. Once people learn your procedures work, they'll support the program.

AN ONGOING SALES EFFORT

Promoting the records management program is not a one-time effort. If records management is to be a success, effort must be applied steadily and consistently. The problem many organizations encounter is that after the initial push to get the program up and running, records management begins to lose priority. Funds and resources are cut; the program loses momentum and effectiveness. After several years of slipping, someone again recognizes that the organization has a "records problem," another major effort is begun, and the cycle starts over again.

It's the records manager's responsibility to insure that the program remains a priority item and does not slip into oblivion. To achieve this goal, you must keep management aware of the program's accomplishments on an ongoing basis. You should also be on the lookout for ways to expand the program and improve its effectiveness.

Ongoing user cooperation is also essential. Users must be aware that you will be responsive to their needs and interested in improving the program whenever possible. When new department heads and records coordinators are appointed, your group should train them in the program instead of letting them assimilate it gradually, and often incorrectly, on their own.

Such ongoing efforts make the company's initial investment in people, time, and money worthwhile and insure the continued effectiveness of the program.

CHAPTER 3

Developing and Staffing the Records Management Program

In the past, records management was one of those functions few people wanted responsibility for. Consequently, the responsibility was often given to whoever did want it, without any consideration as to the function's logical place on the organization chart. Today, organizations are more aware of the importance of their records. Also, automation has added "glamour" to records management. As a result, more thought has been given to the decision on where to position records management, and several options have emerged.

AN ADMINISTRATIVE SERVICES FUNCTION

Ideally, records management belongs in the administrative services area along with such functions as word processing, micrographics, reprographics, telecommunications, and the mail room. Records management, like these other areas, is a support function that crosses departmental lines and provides service throughout the organization. Grouping these similar areas together increases the likelihood that users will receive efficient, comprehensive administrative services from a department that is accustomed to assisting others and perceives such assistance as its primary function.

Also, with the "office of the future" a reality, all the information functions mentioned above can now be closely linked by automation. For example, data keyed into a word processor can now be electronically communicated to an intelligent copier/printer, which can produce "typeset" copies or microfiche. Because of this increasing electronic interaction, it makes sense to group these areas organizationally.

OTHER OPTIONS

The next most likely candidate for the records management responsibility is a relatively new contender—the data processing department, which is often called management information service (MIS). The rationale is that data processing, or MIS, deals with collecting, organizing, and retrieving various types of information, and records management is also involved in these areas. However, although both groups are information-oriented, records management is concerned with the entire life cycle of all organizational information, both hard copy and electronic media. Data processing focuses on electronic information. And in spite of the many articles on the paperless office, most organizations still produce ever increasing amounts of paper records.

Also, although much of the records management process can be automated, much will also remain manual and paper-oriented until legal questions about electronic data are resolved and automation costs are lower. The data processing function usually lacks expertise in the manual systems and legal areas, while the records management group is often inexperienced in the more technical aspects of automation. Consequently, records management and data processing must work as partners in the increasing automation of the records area.

A new trend, most common in those organizations with heavily automated office operations, is the merging of administrative services and data processing into one information services group. With effective management, this group can provide users with the best of both worlds.

A totally unsatisfactory approach is to place records management under the control of either the legal or financial departments. The rationale for the legal department is that this area generates a great many records and also can best set legal retention standards. While legal advice is essential for an effective records management program, problems arise when the total records responsibility rests there. First, lawyers tend to be conservative, and their solution for records retention is often to keep everything forever. Second, it is a waste of a very expensive corporate resource to saddle the legal staff with the responsibility for organizing and managing the company's records—an activity in which they have no particular expertise.

The arguments used to justify placing the records management responsibility under the finance department's authority are similar to those used for justifying the legal department's control. Finance creates a great many important corporate records and is very aware of Internal Revenue Service and other government retention requirements for those records. But while the finance department must be heavily involved in determining the financial importance of various records, this factor hardly qualifies it for overall records responsibility. In fact, the financial staff may even be guilty of "tunnel vision" by perceiving financial records to be more important and more worthy of attention than other records.

Of course, the final alternative is decentralization, with each department assuming complete responsibility for its own records. This approach creates a myriad of problems, including unnecessary duplicate storage of many records, no consistency in filing systems, little or no compliance with legal retention standards, inefficient use of office space and filing equipment, and lost or misplaced information. Individual user departments are not trained in records management, nor is this area a priority to them.

STAFFING THE PROGRAM

Once the basic idea of a central or corporate records management department has been accepted, staffing becomes an important consideration. Records management programs frequently have staffing problems on both the managerial and clerical levels.

On the managerial level, the problem is a definite shortage of qualified records managers. However, if the company is willing to provide sufficient compensation, a qualified records manager can usually be "hired away" from another firm. When bringing in someone from outside, the company may experience not ony resistance to the records management concept but also distrust of a newcomer. Consequently, the person brought in must have strong leadership qualities and the ability to "sell" the program, as well as professional competence in records management.

The other managerial alternative—a very popular one—is to pick someone from within the organization and train him or her to handle the job. This is a reasonable solution. Unlike such fields as accounting and data processing, records management can be learned relatively easily. Of course, the new records manager will need a concentrated training program through seminars and books such as this one. It may also be helpful to hire a consultant to help establish the program and "get it up and running." If you choose this approach, be sure that the records manager helps design the program and feels comfortable managing it after the consultant's work is done.

PROFESSIONAL DEVELOPMENT

If the new records manager is to be successful, he or she should devote considerable time and effort to professional growth and development. Records managers are fortunate that there is a professional association dealing exclusively with their area—the Association of Records Managers and Administrators, Inc. (ARMA). ARMA has over 90 chapters and over 6,000 members. For a modest annual fee, members receive the *Records Management Quarterly,* as well as newsletters and chapter publications. And advertising in these publications is a good way to locate a qualified records manager. Chapter meetings are held regularly, and special workshops and seminars are also offered. But ARMA's most valuable contribution to the records manager is the opportunity to meet and exchange ideas with others in the same profession. You can obtain membership information by writing:

ARMA, Inc.
4200 Somerset, Suite 215
Prairie Village, Kansas 66208

Becoming a Certified Records Manager

Like many other professions, records management has a certification program. To become a Certified Records Manager (CRM), you must have a degree from a four-year accredited college and three years of full-time professional experience in records management or the equivalent, and you must pass a series of examinations on the various aspects of records management. Under certain circumstances, additional years of work experience may be substituted for years of education. Becoming a CRM is difficult and should be attempted only by those individuals planning to make records management their career. Because of the difficulty of obtaining certification, the CRM designation is highly respected and makes advancement within the records management profession much easier. For more information, contact:

Institute of Certified Records Managers
P.O. Box 89
Washington, D.C. 20044

Other Organizations of Interest

Although ARMA is the association of most relevance to the professional records manager, membership in the following groups will also be of great benefit:

Administrative Management Society (AMS)
2360 Maryland Road
Willow Grove, Pennsylvania 19090

National Micrographics Association (NMA)
8710 Colesville Road
Silver Spring, Maryland 20910

Nuclear Records Management Association (NRMA)
P.O. Box 624
Wading River, New York 11792

(The third group is composed of records managers whose companies are involved in nuclear energy—an area with many specialized records problems.)

CLERICAL POSITIONS

Up to now, we've been talking about managerial positions in records management. Now let's turn our attention to the clerical level. Positions such as file clerk, records center clerk, and micrographics camera operator primarily require "on-the-job" training, so finding qualified personnel is relatively easy. Keeping them is another matter.

Several factors are responsible for the high turnover. One is low salaries; other types of work requiring comparable experience often pay better. Also, as their skills improve, the clerical employees move on to better-paying positions. In addition to a low pay scale, the clerical work is usually boring and monotonous. Finally, these positions receive little, if any, respect from others in the company. Remarks like "Have the *girls* check the files" or "Have the *boy* get the box from the records center" are indicative of this problem.

Although these jobs are routine, they are also essential and must be performed well. If there is a continual turnover of file clerks or camera operators, you'll be constantly training new personnel—an expensive and time-consuming process. You'll also have to monitor quality control more closely.

The Solutions

But the situation is not hopeless. By adopting a combination of the strategies outlined below, you can resolve these problems.

The first step is to upgrade both job titles and salaries. According to the Administrative Management Society's *1981–82 Directory of Office Salaries,* a file clerk in the United States receives an average salary of $8,736. Of course, such a salary is a strong incentive to look for another job. At the very least, your records personnel should receive pay comparable to that offered by other companies in the area for similar positions, and ideally the salaries should be greater.

In addition to increasing salaries, job titles should be upgraded and career paths created. For example, a new file clerk might begin as a records analyst trainee and be promoted in three months to a records analyst if the filing systems are mastered. Then, nine months later, he or she could become a senior records analyst and acquire additional responsibilities. For this system to work, the titles must be linked to specific increases in responsibility as well as salary. And the career path should permit qualified individuals to move into supervisory positions when an appropriate opening occurs. One of your best tools for keeping qualified individuals is providing advancement opportunities within the records management area.

Upgrading positions and salaries does not solve the whole problem. In most cases, you also need to make the jobs more interesting. A few people can file or film quite happily all day and do not mind the monotony, but most workers become bored, and the quality of their work suffers.

Two motivational approaches help reduce the monotony. The

first is job enrichment—the technique of having one person per-form several actions that comprise a complete process rather than the same action over and over. As a result, the individual assumes more control over and responsibility for his or her work. Volvo has used this technique successfully by having a team of workers build an entire car, as opposed to the assembly-line method.

Job enrichment can be applied on a smaller scale in records management. For example, instead of having all clerks file throughout the file area, assign portions of the files to various employees and have them each assume responsibility for the main-tenance of their files. This approach tends to increase the employ-ees' interest in their work, as they "learn" an area thoroughly. Filing is done more carefully because employees know they will have to cope with any problems caused by their misfiles. And when errors do occur, you can easily trace them to their source and work with that employee to correct the problem.

Another technique to reduce boredom is cross-training—teach-ing employees to perform more than one job. For example, a file clerk can be taught to film documents. This both breaks the monotony of filing and provides you with a "backup" if the camera operator is on vacation or ill. One caution—some union situations make it difficult or even impossible to cross-train employees.

To further motivate workers, some companies have now formed "quality circles" in the records management area. A quality circle normally consists of up to ten employees and a supervisor or manager. This group usually meets weekly for one hour to discuss ways of improving the department's efficiency or ways to solve problems in the records management area. Remember that the meeting is not a "bitch" session, and discussion should be directed toward potential solutions.

Although the technique has been quite successful, you may initially encounter some reluctance to talk. If so, have each em-ployee write down two or three discussion topics on a piece of paper and turn them in to the supervisor. Selecting key topics from those submitted will provide a good starting point.

Using whatever combination of the above techniques that seems appropriate is one step toward increasing the staff's effectiveness. Another approach many companies have found successful involves using physically or mentally handicapped individuals for various records management positions. For example, operating a rotary microfilm camera is a sedentary job, which can be performed well by someone unable to walk. Preparing documents for microfilming and some types of filing are tasks that some mentally handicapped persons can handle very well.

Hiring handicapped individuals enhances your organization's affirmative action program. Consequently, the personnel department should be able to assist you in finding qualified candidates. One records manager I know checks her organization's disability files periodically for workers receiving disability payments because they are unable to perform strenuous physical work in the warehouse. These individuals are often glad to rejoin the company on an active basis in the records management department. At the same time, the company reduces the number of workers on disability pay.

You will also find shelter workshops and social agencies in your area to be a good source of referrals. Some of these groups will even perform initial training for you (on the operation of a microfilm camera, for example).

Of course, qualified handicapped individuals should move upward along the records management career paths in the same way other department members do.

Another good source of personnel is older individuals who are entering or returning to the workforce. Such people are usually highly motivated, interested in "office work," and looking for an entry-level position with growth possibilities. Job sharing can also be a practical alternative—having two part-time workers perform the duties normally allocated to one full-time position.

One last comment on personnel—whatever the job title or pay scale, your clerical employees should be treated with respect and courtesy, both by you and by others in the company with whom they interact. It's your responsibility to establish a precedent here, by referring to employees by their name or job title, not as the "girls," and by making sure that others within the company treat your staff with similar courtesy.

WHERE TO BEGIN

Now that we've considered where records management belongs in the organization and the proper staffing of the department, you're probably wondering "Where do I start?" As I've already mentioned, you can't institute the entire program at once. The exact order of the steps you choose depends on the current status of records management within the organization. However, the following order is a logical overall approach.

The first step is normally the inventory of records, because until you know what records exist, it is impossible to organize them. Next comes preparing and implementing a retention schedule, because the sooner you destroy obsolete records and transfer inactive records to storage, the easier your remaining tasks will be. After the records' retention values are set, you should identify those records that are vital to the organization's operation and establish a program to protect them.

Then the effectiveness of the organization's active records should be addressed through the improvement and standardization of departmental filing systems. You may even want to establish a central files area for active records. Your last goal is controlling the creation of records through forms management and reports management. When all of these activities are in place and functioning smoothly, records management will be successfully implemented.

Beginning with the next chapter, these topics are covered in the order outlined above. Three other major areas are involved throughout the entire records management process: micrographics, documenting the program through the records manual, and legal considerations. These topics will be discussed separately.

CHAPTER 4

Records Disposition: What to Keep and How Long to Keep It

Why haven't I called this chapter "records retention"? It's true that the term is the traditional name for any program that determines how long specific records should be kept. However, "retention" implies keeping, while "disposition" more accurately suggests taking action and eventually destroying ("disposing of") the records. Consequently, I'll primarily use the term "records disposition" for the remainder of this book.

Whatever name you choose, records retention or disposition is the first step in a complete records management program. Disposition is the first priority because it includes inventorying all the organization's records. And until you know what you have, it's impossible to formulate any type of records program. Disposition is also the first step because it enables you to destroy all unnecessary records. Once you've cleaned out the "deadwood," it's much easier to organize what's left and select appropriate storage and retrieval procedures.

OBJECTIVES

Records disposition accomplishes three objectives. First, it eliminates the costly storage of unneeded records. Second, it provides efficient retrieval of needed, inactive records. And third, it demonstrates the organization's compliance with the legal retention requirements established by federal, state, and local government. By implementing a consistent legal program for disposing of records, the company shows that it is not destroying records on a selective basis to conceal evidence. This third objective—legal compliance—can be of critical importance if the company is involved in litigation.

THE FOUR STEPS

Successfully implementing records disposition is a four-step process. The steps are:

Inventory
Appraisal
Preparation of schedule
Implementation and control

In the remainder of this chapter, we'll examine each step in detail.

INVENTORY

The records inventory determines what records the organization has, where they are located, and how many of them there are. You *cannot* conduct a successful inventory by sending out questionnaires to department heads. Even if they do complete the questionnaires, they are highly unlikely to supply accurate data with all necessary details. For the survey to be of value, it must be a physical inventory conducted by trained members of the records management staff.

Before you panic utterly, the inventory does not mean recording every piece of paper stored in the company or even every different type of document. Instead, you will be identifying every *records series*. A records series is a group of records that are filed together in one system and treated as a unit for disposition purposes. For example, the purchasing department's vendor correspondence is a records series. Such correspondence might be filed first by year and then alphabetically by vendor name for ease in disposition. You would inventory this correspondence as a whole, not folder-by-folder or letter-by-letter. And a year's correspondence would be destroyed *en masse*.

While vendor correspondence or paid invoices are records series consisting of one type of document, some series include several different types. For example, hospital patient records contain a variety of forms and other data. However, each patient file is

treated as a single entity. Consequently, these files would be catego-
rized as one records series.

In addition to the concept of the records series, you need to
remember our definition of a record (Chapter 1). In other words,
you are not inventorying just paper in file folders but also computer
printouts, microfilm, tapes, photographs, slides, drawings—in
short, any recorded information.

Although we've stressed the idea of a comprehensive records
inventory, there is one exception. If the company has a number of
branch locations or field offices performing the same basic functions and keeping similar records, you need only inventory the
records at one or two locations. Otherwise, you'd be "reinventing
the wheel."

What Information to Collect

Before you conduct the inventory, you'll need to prepare a form
for collecting the data you'll need. Figure 1, an example of such a
form, combines both inventory and appraisal information, providing a compact way to collect and organize this data. If you wish, you
may reproduce this form (and all others in this book) for your own
use. Or you may prefer to modify the form to fit your company's
special needs.

A review of the inventory items in Figure 1 will indicate the types
of information you should collect. On the top left blank, write the
official name of the records series—the record title. If more than
one department keeps copies of the records series, be sure that the
same title is used consistently. For example, in different departments, the same records series might be filed as "monthly budget
reports," "summary budget reports," and "budget summaries." An
appropriate standard title would be "Budget Reports—Monthly."

A separate inventory card should be prepared for each department that has copies of this record, and the appropriate department should be identified on the top line of the inventory/appraisal
form. If the records series contains only one particular kind of
form or report, then the form or report number should also be
given.

Once the top identification line is completed, you can gather the
necessary information for the left-hand, or inventory, side of the
form. Here you'll need to determine whether you are inventorying

RECORDS INVENTORY/APPRAISAL

Record Title			Dept.			Form No. (If Any)	

INVENTORY

☐ Copy of record   ☐ Duplicate

Years	Volume	Filing Method

TYPE OF FILING EQUIPMENT

☐ Vertical letter   ☐ Open shelf
☐ Vertical legal   ☐ Automated
☐ Lateral   ☐ Other _____

OTHERS WITH COPIES (IF KNOWN)

ACTIVITY LEVEL/OTHER REMARKS

Inventoried by _____ Date

APPRAISALS

Name	Date	Years
ADMINISTRATIVE		Office
		Stor.
LEGAL		
FISCAL/TAX		
ARCHIVAL		

Remarks

Final Schedule

Office	Storage
Authorized by	Date

Figure 1. Records inventory/appraisal form.

the *copy of record* or a duplicate copy. The copy of record is the "official" organization copy. When this copy is no longer needed in the office, it will be placed in inactive storage at the company's records center for the remainder of its life span. Duplicate copies, however, are only kept in the office for as long as they are needed and then destroyed.

The next question, of course, is "How do you determine which copy is the copy of record?" There is no one answer that always works, but the following guidelines will resolve the issue:

If the original is kept within the company, it normally becomes the copy of record.

If the original is not kept within the company (a letter, for example), then the originator's copy becomes the copy of record.

If neither of the above conditions is met, then the copy of record is the copy belonging to the department that has the greatest need and use for the record.

Next on the form is space for current statistics on the records series, starting with "Years." For example, if the purchasing department has all 1978–82 vendor correspondence in the office, you'd enter "1978–82" under "Years."

Volume can be measured either in filing inches (number of inches of the record) or cubic feet. To compute cubic feet, use the following rule: When full, a letter-sized file drawer contains 1.5 cubic feet of records, while a legal-sized drawer holds 2 cubic feet. Filing inches are easier for the person inventorying to compute, especially when a variety of types of filing equipment are used. However, cubic feet are more accurate, as legal- and letter-sized file drawers hold the same number of filing inches but different amounts of cubic feet. Either measurement system is acceptable for inventorying, but the same system should be used consistently throughout the inventory.

On the inventory/appraisal form, "filing method" refers to the alphabetic or numeric system the department uses to organize a particular records series. And, of course, "filing equipment" refers to the type of cabinet the records are stored in. The different types of filing systems and filing equipment are discussed in Chapter 7.

Listing other departments known to have copies of the record makes it easier to determine which copy should be the copy of record and also insures that all departments' retention needs for that records series are considered. Under the "Activity Level/Other Remarks" section, you can jot down any pertinent comments about how frequently the records are referred to, who maintains the files, and so on. If you're using filing inches to measure volume, it's a good idea to give the records' physical size here, such as 4" × 6" cards.

Tips on Inventorying

Top management should notify all departments, in advance, about the inventory, emphasizing its purpose and importance. It's usually a good idea to draft the memo yourself for the appropriate executive's approval and signature. Such executives tend to be very busy, and if you wait for one of them to write the memo, it may never get written.

Conducting a records inventory is, in some ways, a public relations effort. The inventory may prompt both resentment and paranoia. Consequently, courtesy, sensitivity, and persistence are needed to get the job done.

As one such courtesy, schedule the inventories at times that are convenient for the various departments. (But don't accept the excuse that no time is convenient.) Be sure that both the department heads and the secretaries or others responsible for file maintenance will be in the office during the inventory. Then if you have a question about the files, a qualified individual will be present to answer it. By the way, all inventorying should be done in the presence of a department staff member; this practice prevents misunderstanding and insures that neither you nor a member of your staff will be accused of misplacing or removing records.

Persistence is often necessary to insure that you've located *all* of the department's records. Of course, you'll physically check all file cabinets. But in many departments, that's only the beginning. Check closets and storage cabinets, as well as any "suspicious" cardboard cartons or large boxes. Don't forget computer printout racks and card files.

The most questionable area is an employee's desk files. Obviously, any file cabinet in an employee's office should be inventoried. However, active working files on or in an employee's desk are not surveyed, as they have not yet entered the department's filing system. Employees' "personal" files are also not usually surveyed. However, it's a good idea to have employees pull all completed files from their desks and incorporate them into the department's other records.

Two final inventorying tips—it's a good idea to affix colored, self-adhesive dots to each file drawer, carton, and so forth, after it's inventoried. Then if you are temporarily interrupted, you can easily resume where you left off. And, finally, you may want to print the inventory/appraisal form on 5½" × 8½" card stock for increased durability and ease in handling and filing.

THE FILE EQUIPMENT SURVEY

When you inventory each department's records, you should also survey its filing equipment. The records disposition program should "free up" a number of pieces of filing equipment, which may need to be redistributed within the organization. Figure 2 is a sample form that can be used to inventory filing equipment. The form is self-explanatory and should be completed for each department. For detailed descriptions of the various types of filing equipment, see Chapter 7.

Frequently, completion of the disposition process leaves more filing equipment empty than the organization can use in the near future. Instead of selling this equipment to a vendor of used office furniture, you might consider offering it to employees on a highest bid basis. Not only will the company probably make more money this way, but the sale will also build goodwill. You'll find many employees could use a file cabinet or two for their family records but don't want or can't afford to purchase a new one. Another option is donating some of the equipment to a local charity. In addition to maintaining good public relations, the company receives a tax deduction.

THE APPRAISAL

After the inventory is complete, the records must be appraised—not for their monetary worth, but for their value to the organization and, in particular, for the length of time they should be kept.

FILE EQUIPMENT SURVEY

Dept./Location		Inventoried by		Date

TYPE	Number In Use	Number Empty	Letter	Legal	Lock	No Lock	Remarks
Vertical 2 drawer							
3 drawer							
4 drawer							
5 drawer							
Lateral 2 drawer							
3 drawer							
4 drawer							
5 drawer							
Open Shelf							
Compactable							
Automated							
Card File							
Printout Cabinet							
Other							

Figure 2. File equipment survey form.

As part of the appraisal process, four types of value must be considered for each record. They are:

Administrative value
Legal value
Fiscal value
Historical or archival value

Let's examine each separately to see how it is determined and who determines it.

Administrative Value

The administrative value is the length of time the record may be needed or used within the company. This value is usually set by the department head who is responsible for the copy of record, although the needs of other departments using the record should also be considered.

In addition to an overall retention value, the department head should also set a period of active use. For this period, the record will be kept in the office; then, it will go to the records center for the remainder of the retention period. For most records, the active period should not exceed two years, and it may be substantially less. Of course, there are exceptions, such as an employee's benefit file, which remains active as long as the employee is with the company.

The administrative appraisal, as well as the other appraisal values, can be recorded on the right-hand side of Figure 1, the records inventory/appraisal form.

Legal Value

How long the company needs a record is one thing. How long the government thinks you should keep it is another. There are over 1,000 federal statutes and regulations governing records retention, plus a variety of state and local legislation. And no government or court will accept ignorance of a regulation as a satisfactory excuse for noncompliance.

Some companies simply adopt a "suggested" or "recommended" retention schedule that has been prepared by a vendor or consultant for general use. This approach is not advisable because different types of companies are accountable to different regulatory agencies. As a result, two companies may have different retention requirements for the same record. Also, state and local requirements vary widely, and the company must comply with the retention requirements for each state in which it does business. Consequently, the company's legal department should appraise each records series to determine whether it has a legal retention period and, if so, how long.

Legal appraisals are further complicated by the fact that government agencies set their retention requirements autonomously. That is, one agency may specify a three-year period, another six years, and a third may say "as long as seems appropriate." Normally you have to comply with the longest of the periods, although "as long as seems appropriate" may be taken to mean the administrative retention value. This situation should improve in the next few years as the Paperwork Reduction Act of 1980 is fully implemented. (See Chapter 12 for a detailed discussion of the Act.)

In the interim, your best help is the *Guide to Record Retention Requirements*, published annually by the Office of the Federal Register. This booklet summarizes over 1,000 federal retention requirements and can be ordered for a nominal charge by writing:

Superintendent of Documents
U.S. Government Printing Office
Washington, D.C. 20402

For information on state retention requirements, contact your state "records office" or "archivist" (titles vary from state to state).

Occasionally, a legal department unfamiliar with records management takes the position that if the company keeps everything permanently, it will definitely be in compliance with all retention regulations. That's true, but this is a very costly form of compliance. First, there is the expense of storing the records. Second, if the company is sued, it will be required to produce everything it has relating to the suit. And if everything's been kept, the cost of finding and reproducing all appropriate documents may be substantial.

If your legal department needs some additional motivation, refer it to "Document Retention and Destruction: Practical, Legal and Ethical Considerations," in the October 1980 issue of *The Notre Dame Lawyer* (available through ARMA). This article, by John M.

Fedders and Lauryn H. Guttenplan, presents a comprehensive analysis of records retention from a lawyer's point of view.

Fiscal Value

Some records also have a fiscal value. Consequently, you should ask a qualified individual from the finance department, such as the controller, to determine whether each records series is important from a fiscal or tax standpoint and, if so, to assign a retention period. Obviously, such retention values should comply with the regulatory requirements of agencies such as the Internal Revenue Service and the Securities and Exchange Commission, as well as the company's own audit requirements.

Historical Value

Records can also have historical or archival value. You may remember the recent republishing of an early Sears, Roebuck catalog. Although the information in that catalog no longer had legal, fiscal, or administrative value, it was definitely of historical interest. For this same reason, firms often keep copies of advertisements, company publications, and other similar material of historical or archival interest. Usually the records manager (or corporate archivist, if there is one), in conjunction with a representative of top management, determines if a record has historical value.

SETTING THE FINAL RETENTION VALUE

Normally the longest of the four retention values is assigned to the records series as its official retention period. One caution, though—many department heads assign unrealistic administrative retention values. They want to keep everything for at least 50 years, or so it seems. If the administrative retention value is significantly longer than the other three values, ask the department head why he or she needs the record so long.

And if you're not satisfied with the answer, begin negotiating for a more realistic time frame. An effective tactic is to keep the records as requested for a year and measure the retrieval activity for that period. Then if the older records have not been referred to, you have a legitimate basis for arguing for a shorter retention period.

For example, assume the marketing director wants to keep some reports for ten years, and the legal retention requirement is five years. Measure the reports' usage for a year. If no one has referred to the oldest five years' copies in that time, recommend a seven-year retention period, citing the lack of usage as support. If another year of no usage occurs, then it's time to cut back to the five-year requirement.

You may also need to effect similar reductions in office storage periods. Normally records should be kept in the office for one to two years, so you should question most longer periods and gradually negotiate them back to two years. As users realize that they don't refer to extremely old records and that they can quickly obtain inactive records from storage, they will become more receptive to shorter retention periods. Your ultimate goal should be to shorten most retention periods to the legal, fiscal, or archival requirements. Be patient, though; it takes time and proof that the records aren't being referred to to convince users to accept shorter retention periods.

PREPARING THE RETENTION SCHEDULE

After the retention periods are established and approved, it's a relatively simple matter to prepare a schedule using a form similar to Figure 3. Usually the records series are first grouped either by subject (such as accounting) or by primary user department. Then they are listed alphabetically in these groupings. Categorizing the records by subject instead of department is more logical because a record could be used heavily by several departments, leading to either repetitious or confusing listings. Small organizations often find a simple alphabetical listing by records series title adequate without any preliminary subject breakdowns.

On the retention schedule, the record title should be its official name. However, in large organizations, different groups may refer to the same record by a variety of names. In such instances, a brief description of the record, after its "official" title, may be appropriate. Of course, if the record has a unique report or form number, that will eliminate confusion and should be listed.

The retention schedule should also include the media on which the records are stored. Typical categories include paper, microfilm, or magnetic media such as computer tapes, disks, or diskettes. If

RECORDS DISPOSITION SCHEDULE

Subject	Date Effective		Page 10
ACCOUNTING	8/20/83		

Record Title	Form or Report No.	Media	Vital	Dept. with Copy	Retention in Years	
					Office	Storage
Expense Reports, Employee	3791-B	paper		Finance Employee	1 1 or less	6

Figure 3. Records disposition schedule.

the record is "vital" (necessary to resume operations in the event of a disaster), a check mark appears in the appropriate column. Chapter 6 discusses vital records in detail.

Some companies also indicate which copy is the "copy of record" on the retention schedule. However, since by our definition the copy of record must be the copy sent to storage, designating it as such is repetitious. Likewise, it's redundant to give total years kept in addition to years in office and in storage.

If more than one copy of a record exists within the company, each copy should be listed with an appropriate retention period. Of course, only the copy of record will have a storage retention period. Duplicate copies will have brief in-office storage periods (normally one year or less). Listing each copy will eliminate any confusion as to how long a particular record is kept. Otherwise, in Figure 3, employees might think they should keep their copies of the expense report seven years. Also, the separate listing insures that company "pack rats" do not keep their duplicate copies for excessive periods.

INTRODUCING RECORDS DISPOSITION

The department records coordinators (see Chapter 2) are your most valuable aid in introducing the disposition program. You or you staff should train the coordinators in the program. Then they can make sure that their departments' records are sent to storage or destroyed in accordance with the new schedule.

When you introduce the program, you may need to initially assign each department a one- or two-week period for sending inactive records to storage. Otherwise, everyone's records may arrive at the records center simultaneously, to the dismay of the center personnel.

CONTROLLING THE PROGRAM

Although most departments will begin records disposition conscientiously, as time passes, you'll have some "backsliders." To insure that the program remains effective, you'll need to institute control techniques.

Ideally, each department should have its files audited annually, either by the internal audit function or by the records management staff. An important part of the audit is determining if the department is complying with the retention schedule. (See Chapter 7 for a detailed discussion of files audits.)

Although audits are ideal, you may not always have the resources to conduct them. Fortunately, there is a simple, effective control technique that every organization can follow. Just have management establish a policy that all requests for new filing equipment must be approved by the records manager. Before approving a request, you then check to make sure the department is complying with the records disposition schedule.

Sometimes you don't even need to check. One records manager I know received a request from the legal department for ten new file cabinets. She replied with a memo explaining that she couldn't approve the request unless the department was in compliance with the retention schedule. Two days later, 40 cartons of legal records arrived at the records center, and the request for new file cabinets was withdrawn.

If your records center has a computerized indexing system, it's a simple matter to obtain a printout listing those departments that have not sent records to storage within the past year. You can then follow up with these departments to insure compliance.

ANNUAL REVIEWS

In addition to insuring that all areas of the company comply with the schedule, you must also keep the schedule current. Each year all records series should be reappraised, and whenever possible, retention values should be reduced. Legal and fiscal retention requirements change, and only an annual review will insure that all of these changes are reflected in the schedule. And as mentioned earlier, usage records may reveal that some administrative retention standards can be reduced. However, I would only reappraise a record's historical value when that value is the longest retention period. Once set, historical retention values remain fairly constant.

Annual reviews serve another purpose. They keep records retention fresh in everyone's mind and make it clear that the organization is committed to the program on an ongoing basis. When a schedule is never revised, people begin to distrust it. They suspect, quite rightly, that the standards set five or ten years ago are no longer appropriate, and they start disregarding the schedule.

Not only should the retention periods for existing records be reexamined, but any new records series should be added to the schedule. The records coordinators should notify the records manager of any new records series in their departments. Files audits are also useful for uncovering new records series. The new series are then inventoried and appraised in the manner described earlier in this chapter.

TYPICAL RESULTS

Implementing a comprehensive records disposition program will "free up" substantial amounts of office space and filing equipment. Consider the following statistics from an ARMA survey. On an average, 24.1 percent of the total volume of a company's records are destroyed when a retention program is begun. Another 32.3 percent of the records are sent to inactive storage in a records center. And only 43.6 percent of the records remain in the office area. In other words, over half of the office space occupied by records can be used for people or office equipment such as copiers and word processors.

CHAPTER 5

The Records Center

In records management, the term "records center" is used to indicate "a central storage area for the company's inactive records"—those records that must be kept but are not used frequently enough to justify high-cost office storage. Although some companies use the term "records center" to indicate a central file room for active records, that usage is incorrect and creates confusion. Likewise, the inactive records storage area is sometimes incorrectly referred to as the company archives. In reality, an archives is a special storage area for the permanent preservation of documents of historical significance.

Because they are designed for inactive records, records centers should provide cheap storage while permitting relatively prompt retrieval. Meeting these dual objectives means that records centers are visually unexciting—even ugly—and totally functional.

RECORDS CENTER ALTERNATIVES

A company has four alternatives for storing inactive records:

An on-site center
A separate off-site facility
Leased warehouse space
A commercial records center

Let's examine the pros and cons of each option.

On-Site Storage

Storing inactive records on-site is a common practice for small to medium-size companies that have available space within their buildings. Usually these companies own their buildings and are located in areas with comparatively inexpensive real estate. For example, it would hardly be economical to rent additional space in midtown Manhattan for storing inactive records. But if the company owns a building with basement space to spare, an on-site center might be the best and cheapest means of storage.

Usually on-site centers are located on the basement or ground floor, so that the weight of the records does not strain the building unduly. Also, transferring records in and out of the building is simplified because elevators are not involved. An on-site records center should have adequate fire protection, security, and lighting, as well as all the other physical characteristics of records centers that are discussed later in this chapter. The on-site center is *not* a large storeroom for departmental Christmas decorations or other infrequently used items. The center should be used only for records.

A Separate Records Center

Large organizations often build or lease totally separate records center buildings. Building such a facility is practical and cost-effective only for the largest organizations. The federal government has several records centers, as do many oil and utility companies. These centers have been carefully planned to use space and equipment most effectively.

Depending on the facilities available in the area, leasing an entire warehouse may be a practical option for the company with an extensive inactive records collection. While the physical characteristics of the building may not be the optimum combination for a records center, the cost benefits of leasing may outweigh any building limitations.

Warehouse Space

For the company that does not need a separate records center building and does not have space available in its building, leasing warehouse space and leasing records center space are the two choices.

Warehouse space is the cheaper of the two leasing options. Here the company rents space in a commercial warehouse such as those owned by moving and storage companies. The only service provided is bringing cartons into and out of the warehouse at your request. Your company is responsible for indexing its records, determining which box should be retrieved, destroying records when their retention period expires, and so forth.

One problem with these facilities is that the retrieval process is usually somewhat involved. The warehouse must be notified in advance, and a company representative must go pick up the records. Because retrieval is complex and time-consuming, users tend to resist storing their records in the warehouse.

Another problem is the "out of sight, out of mind" syndrome. Because the records are not maintained actively by company personnel, they are often forgotten and not destroyed in accordance with the retention schedule.

The Commercial Records Center

The commercial records center is a more desirable (and more expensive) leasing alternative. These facilities are designed exclusively for records storage and provide a wide range of services, which vary from center to center. For example, the commercial center will place in storage, retrieve, and destroy records at your request. Some centers will retrieve individual records from a box, while others will retrieve only the entire box.

Many commercial centers have computer indexing systems that will speed retrieval and notify you when records are due for destruction. Commercial centers also have environmentally controlled areas for storing magnetic media and microfilm. Some centers also have vaults for storing vital records. (See Chapter 6 for more information on vital records.)

Usually, commercial centers' charges are based on the services they provide. Thus, there is a monthly charge for each carton stored, a separate charge for each instance of retrieving or refiling records, and a charge for the destruction or permanent removal of records. Some centers allow you to use your own cartons, while others require that you use theirs and usually charge you for the cartons.

When selecting a commercial records center, visit all available facilities in your area. Check references carefully. Getting opinions from other ARMA members in your area who use commercial centers is also a good idea. Your prime concerns should be:

Speed of retrieval. Here check not only how quickly records are pulled but also the center's operating hours and the simplicity of the retrieval process.

Will they retrieve items from a carton or only the entire carton? With confidential material, you won't want the center staff to open boxes. With other records, you may prefer having the center "pull" individual items, so you won't have to cope with an entire box back at the office. This practice also reduces the chance of records being lost.

Will they deliver records or do you have to pick them up? While you may not always want to use the more expensive delivery, there are times when it's a real convenience.

Fire protection provisions. The building should be fire-resistant. Also, the center should have an internal fire-fighting system. Some centers use chemical fire-extinguishing systems because of the extensive water damage sprinklers cause.

Security. The center should have a burglar alarm system and other appropriate security measures, as well as adequate controls to insure that unauthorized persons cannot obtain records under false pretenses.

An on-site work area available to your company. At times, someone from your company may need to "browse" through several boxes of records in order to locate an item. In these circumstances, it can be inconvenient and time-consuming to have the boxes delivered to the company and then returned.

Indexing capabilities. Check to see whether or not the center provides either computerized or manual indexing and, if so, how sophisticated the system is. We'll discuss both types of systems later in this chapter.

Cost. You should compare costs carefully for those centers you are seriously considering using. Pay special attention to the charge for permanently removing your records. Some centers have a very high charge for permanent removal. This charge is designed to make it difficult for you to cost-justify removing your records, even though you are unhappy with the center's service or have located a less expensive center. However, if you are using a center with a high permanent removal fee and are dissatisfied, don't be discouraged. Some centers will agree to pay the removal fee if you decide to move your records to their facility.

One last tip—it's a good idea to "test" the center you select for a few months. Send over one or two departments' inactive records before you make a major commitment.

CENTER DESIGN

Both company-operated and commercial records centers tend to be remarkably similar in physical design. Moreover, the design guidelines have changed relatively little in the past 20 years for a simple reason—no one has found a better way.

When the records center has its own special building, the facility is generally a single-level concrete structure with windows limited to office and entry areas. Such a structure provides good security and fire protection. The building's ceiling is generally at least 15 feet high to allow maximum use of space through shelving tiers and stacked cartons. Obviously, an on-site center will probably have lower ceilings. Also, with an on-site operation, you may not be able to have a windowless storage area. In such an instance, you should, however, arrange for bars, grates, or other security precautions.

In addition to an area for records storage, the center should have adequate office space for its staff and work areas for center users. Just as in a commercial center, individuals may need to browse through one or more cartons. Having a work area means the cartons don't have to leave the center and allows users to request other cartons easily.

When microfilm, magnetic media, or archival documents are stored in the center, temperature and humidity should be strictly controlled. Otherwise, if the climate permits, a good ventilation and heating system may suffice. In any case, the offices and work areas should be air-conditioned for the comfort of their users.

Good fire protection is essential for any records center. Most larger centers have sprinkler systems, although a few have chemical fire-extinguishing systems. Fire walls are often constructed between sections of large centers to prevent a fire from spreading. Some records centers have vaults to protect microfilm and vital records from fire damage.

Even more important than protecting the records from fire is protecting the center's employees. While for security reasons, there may be only one entrance to the records center, ideally there should be other fire exits. Emergency procedures should be reviewed carefully with all center employees and fire drills conducted regularly. Of course, the best and wisest precaution of all is a strictly enforced no-smoking rule in the records center.

Although fire is the most obvious danger, records centers do have the potential for a variety of accidents. Falls from ladders, back injuries due to improper lifting procedures, and forklift truck accidents are a few possibilities. To minimize risk, have the company's safety or OSHA expert inspect the center and make appropriate suggestions.

The records center should have phone service, so users can "call in" requests for records. Good lighting is also important, with fluorescent lights most commonly used. If possible, the lighting system should be wired so that the lights in each aisle and/or section can be turned on and off separately to conserve energy.

CARTONS AND SHELVING

For the actual storage of the records, a combination of standard-size cartons and steel shelving will keep costs down, use space efficiently, and permit quick retrieval. For these reasons, many records centers use a system similar or identical to the one outlined below.

The standard storage container is made of corrugated cardboard with a "shoe box" style lift-off lid and handholes for ease in carrying. The carton is 15 inches long, 12 inches wide, and 10 inches high. This versatile container can hold legal-size files along the 15-inch length and letter-size files along the 12-inch width. The cartons are designed to be stored flat when not in use to reduce storage space and can be assembled easily.

I recommend that you avoid the combination corrugated-and-steel pull-out file units that are stacked on top of each other. Some users experience difficulty in opening drawers near the bottom of the stack and find that the units do not wear well.

Typically the shelving is steel, although particle board shelving is also available and is less expensive. If you consider particle board shelves, avoid those made with formaldehyde. Problems have occurred from such shelving's emitting injurious fumes.

The shelving units are usually 42 inches wide and 30 inches deep,

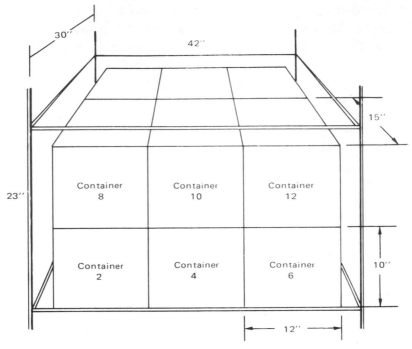

Figure 4. Shelving with records containers.

with 23 inches between shelves. With these dimensions, each shelf can hold 12 cartons (3 across, 2 deep, and 2 high) as shown in Figure 4. A six-shelf unit will hold 72 standard containers in approximately 17 square feet including aisle space. The same records would occupy approximately 60 square feet of office space in conventional filing equipment.

Usually the aisles between the rows of shelves are 2½ feet to 3 feet wide. The main "feeder" aisles are often 5 feet to 6 feet wide, depending on the type of equipment (forklift truck, pushcart, and so on) that must pass down them. Some newer forklift trucks can maneuver in 4-foot aisles.

ORGANIZING THE RECORDS

To use available space most effectively, don't segregate records in the center by department. Instead place the cartons in any available space and assign box numbers to denote the locations. (Of course, you wouldn't mix more than one department's records within a box.) To retrieve a particular record, the center staff simply checks the index to determine the box number and then locates the record accordingly. An additional advantage to this system is improved security because the boxes are only numbered and not labeled as to their contents.

Numbering systems vary in complexity according to the extent of the organization's records. Usually the first number or letter indicates the row of shelving, the second the section or unit of shelving within that row, the third the particular shelf, and the fourth the specific box.

For example, the number "5-3-6-10" tells us row 5, section 3 (sections are usually numbered from the main aisle inward), shelf 6 (start at the bottom with shelf one), and box 10. Odd numbered boxes are on the back row and even-numbered ones on the front, as shown in Figure 4. The lower 6 boxes are numbered first, so box one is in the back on the bottom to the left, box 2 is at the front on the bottom to the left, box 3 is at the back on the bottom next to box one, and so on. Box 7 is at the back on top of box one, box 8 on top of box 2, and so on.

If you wish, you can use letters instead of numbers for some of the location categories, such as row and shelf. Under this system, row 5 would be row E and shelf 6, shelf F. Our sample location number would then be "E3-F10." If you're planning to computerize the center's index, you'll need to make sure the numbering system presents no programming problems. For example, you'll want to use zeros as placeholders for boxes with one-digit numbers (that is, 01, 02, and so on).

INDEXING

An index is essential for the successful operation of any records center. Users should not be required to supply box numbers when they request a record, and boxes should need to be labeled only with an identifying number.

Indexing capabilities and retrieval speed have greatly improved with the advent of automated systems. Many organizations either have computerized or are in the process of computerizing their records center indexes. And if it's at all practical and cost-effective given the company's size and resources, you should automate yours also. Automation not only saves labor, but it also makes the data in the records center much more accessible. Consequently, the bulk of our discussion of indexing will focus on automated indexing systems, although a simple and effective manual system will also be described.

Computerized Indexing

The potential capabilities of an automated indexing system include:

1. *Giving the correct location of any record stored in the center.* Some systems index individual documents by a variety of data fields such as subject, date, author, type of document, and so on. With such a system, you could quickly locate all letters on environmental protection written by a particular plant manager in 1979. Such highly sophisticated systems are advantageous for large organizations— particularly those that are heavily regulated and may have to quickly produce all existing documentation on a specific topic for a government agency. Other organizations find an indexing system that identifies in general terms the contents of a carton and locates records series by title and year to be adequate. And of course, these systems are less costly.

2. *Assuring compliance with retention schedules.* The computer tells the records center staff which records should be destroyed each month. The computer can also print out notifications of pending destruction to be sent to the appropriate department heads. Logically, department heads should not need to be notified prior to the destruction of their records. They should realize that the company will automatically follow the retention schedule. However, "pending destruction" notices give users a feeling of security; they know no record will be destroyed without their knowledge. Consequently they are more willing to entrust their records to the center.

Send out the destruction notices 30 days before the records are to be destroyed. The notice should state that if you do not hear to the contrary within that time period, the records will automatically be destroyed. Requiring department heads to sign a form authorizing destruction slows down the whole process and diminishes the effectiveness of the entire retention schedule. Of course, department heads should not be allowed to postpone destruction without a good reason. If there is a repeated need for postponement, the schedule should be changed accordingly, not continually disregarded.

The legal department should also receive notification of all records to be destroyed. This important precaution protects the company's interests. If the records are needed for a court case, destruction will have to be postponed, regardless of the schedule.

3. *Providing users with an index of their holdings in the records center.* Manually preparing such indexes would be tedious and costly; the computer can do them quickly and update them easily. This service is especially helpful for new department heads who might not know what records they've "inherited." It also serves as an additional "security blanket" for nervous department heads who are afraid their records are lost forever once they go to the center.

4. *Allocating storage costs to the various user departments.* Many companies charge users of the center a "per box" storage fee. Admittedly, this practice doesn't make any money for the company, and it does add to the accounting process. But more importantly, when department heads "pay" for their storage space, they recognize what it actually costs the company to store their records. Then they are more receptive to reducing retention periods and saving money on their own budgets.

5. *Keeping a current inventory of available storage space for incoming material.* When a box of records is destroyed, that fact is entered into the computer. That space or box number is then listed as being available for new records. Keeping track of available space manually is tedious, and open spaces can easily be overlooked. Computerization solves that problem.

6. *Preparing regular activity reports for each year of each records series.* These reports on each records series' usage provide valuable documentation for reducing retention periods when appropriate. They may also reveal certain still active records that should be kept in the office area longer.

7. *Providing cross-referencing capabilities.* With a computerized system, it's easy to identify records by their synonyms, as well as by their official records series titles. For large organizations whose records are known by a variety of names, this capability is a real

time-saver. Likewise, forms and reports can be located by their numbers as well as by their official titles.

8. *Producing summary reports on the number of boxes added, deleted, and still in storage.* Such reports make it easy for you to track the increasing amount of records in storage (and it will increase!). Then you can project future needs in personnel and space. You'll also use this data to determine the correct "per box" fee to charge users of the center.

You can also generate summary reports on the number of retrievals and refiles. You can then determine the average workload one individual can be expected to handle. This data will help you plan your staffing requirements. These summary reports can also be used to determine seasonal peak periods of center usage, when you may need additional staff to meet user demands.

The exact way you achieve these eight objectives will depend on the size of the records collection and the computer's capabilities. The data processing staff will be responsible for determining the best way to program the computer to meet your objectives. With the advent of mini- and microcomputers, some companies have chosen to use one of these options as opposed to the company's mainframe computer. If you do elect to use a mini- or microcomputer, be sure to consider compatibility with other terminals in the system. Eventually you'll want your terminal to "communicate" with others, and if you haven't planned carefully, the equipment may be incompatible.

Whatever the hardware, if possible, choose a system that allows your staff to enter the appropriate data on new records directly into the computer, instead of filling out cards or forms for the data processing staff to code into the computer. The more control you and your staff have over the indexing system, the happier you will be.

Manual Indexing

If automated indexing is not feasible at this time, you'll need to develop a manual system. The procedure is a simple one. Each records series has an index card similar to the example in Figure 5. When any records in the series are received at the records center, the following information is entered on the appropriate index card:

Record Title			Dept. Received From						
Date Received	Received By	Box Number	Contents				Date To Be Destroyed	Date Destroyed	Certified By
			Alpha. or Num.		Date				
			From	To	From	To			

Figure 5. Records center index card

The date received.

Who accepted the records. (If a problem should arise, this information can be very useful.)

The box number (which also gives the record's location if you use a system like the one outlined earlier in this chapter).

The date to destroy the records (based on the disposition schedule).

While this system does not provide as much information as its automated counterpart, it does provide a simple, effective way to locate records.

To insure that the records are destroyed on schedule, you can set up a simple monthly log or card file for as many years into the future as necessary. Then when records are added to the index card, their box numbers are also entered in the log under the appropriate month and year for destruction, such as January 1988. Each month, the log is checked and the appropriate departments notified of the pending destructions. Thirty days later, the boxes are destroyed. The destruction is recorded on the index card so no one will attempt to find records that have been destroyed.

TRANSFERRING RECORDS TO THE CENTER

In addition to a comprehensive indexing system, the records center needs simple, effective procedures for transferring records to the center and retrieving them when needed. Let's consider the transfer process first.

The first steps in the transfer process are the responsibility of the department whose records will be stored. The department requests the required number of boxes from the records center or supply room. To save space, the empty boxes are stored and delivered in a collapsed form. Department personnel then assemble the boxes and fill them. The boxes should be the same cartons in which the records will actually be stored—not the reusable "transfer boxes" you may have seen advertised. Transfer boxes simply make more work for the records center staff, who must then reload the records in standard cartons. The various departments are perfectly capable of packing their records correctly; let them do it.

To determine how many boxes the department needs, remember

this rule: One legal-size drawer requires two standard boxes (12″ × 15″ × 10″); two letter-size drawers require three boxes. If the users are not transferring the records from vertical file drawers, have them measure the number of inches of records. A box holds 15 inches of letter-size files or 12 inches of legal-size, so calculating the appropriate number of boxes is a simple matter.

After the boxes are filled, the user department completes a transfer list similar to the one in Figure 6. Be sure to have the department assign temporary numbers to each box (1 of 5, 2 of 5, and so on). These numbers should be written both on the boxes and on the transfer list. By using the ___ of ___ approach, the records center staff can easily determine if they've received all of the cartons, even if the list becomes lost or separated from the boxes.

The department sends two copies of the transfer list with the boxes and keeps the third copy. The records center staff fills in the permanent box numbers and sends one copy of the form back to the user department. The third copy of the form is then destroyed. Thus, the user department always has a copy of the list for its records. Now, admittedly, it's repetitious to give the department the permanent box numbers, since the index contains this information. However, most users have much more confidence in the system if they know exactly where their records are and do not have to depend on the records center for that information. Also, returning the copy lets the users know that their records arrived safely.

To insure that the records center is not misused, the center staff should only accept records series that are listed on the retention schedule. If you do not establish this rule, you'll find that you're storing duplicate copies of the same records series for different departments, as well as storing records that have no inactive storage value.

WHEN TO TRANSFER RECORDS

One remaining problem is when a department should send its records to the center. If you answer "as soon as the active usage period is over," think again. Let's assume we have a correspondence file with a one-year active retention period followed by two years inactive storage. Now at the end of the year, we have one year's correspondence filed together. Some of the letters are a year old;

RECORDS TRANSFER LIST						
1. Send first two copies of this form with boxed records to Records Center. 2. When you receive the second copy back with the permanent box numbers, destroy the third copy.						
Dept. From				**Date Sent**		
Temporary Box No. — of —	**Record Title**	Contents				Permanent Box No. (Assigned by Records Center)
		Alpha./Num.		Date		
		From	To	From	To	
Date Received at Center			By Whom			

Figure 6. Records transfer list.

others may have been written or received within the past week and may need to be referred to frequently. So a part of the file meets the retention period, but part does not. Continual purging of year-old letters from the file is, of course, impractical and inefficient.

The solution to our dilemma is known as the *minimum-maximum method.* Instead of sending the 1981 correspondence to the records center at the end of the year, we hold it in the office until June 1982. Of course, we also set up a 1982 correspondence file at the beginning of the year. Sending the correspondence to the center in June means that the records are kept in the office a minimum of 6 months (the December 1981 letters) and a maximum of 18 months (the January 1981 letters). The average active retention period is one year.

As you can see, the minimum-maximum effectively solves the problem. But if you're not careful, it can cause another problem— namely, the records center staff will be inundated with records at certain times of the year. To avoid this situation, set up a system with the various departmental records coordinators so that the departments will send their records to the center at different times. June doesn't have to be the month. For less frequently used records, earlier months such as April and May might work very well. For more frequently referenced records, you might try later months.

RETRIEVING RECORDS

If users are to have confidence in the records center, you'll need to establish a fast, simple retrieval procedure. Users should normally be able to request a record in four different ways: by phone, interdepartmental mail, personal visit, or messenger. (In the case of an off-site center, a personal visit may be impractical.)

A simple three-part form similar to Figure 7 should be available to users for requesting records. Figure 7 is basically self-explanatory, with the exception of the "remarks" space at the bottom. Here records center personnel can indicate if they had any difficulty locating the record, if the requester supplied incorrect information, or if the record could not be found. Admittedly, the last option could be covered by a check box on the form, but it's bad public relations to openly admit that possibility.

RECORDS REQUEST		
To be completed by requesting department. **Send all copies to Records Center.**		
Record Title	Dept. Requesting	
Record Date	Send To	
Box No. (Not Required)	Phone No.	
Record Detail		
To be completed by Records Center.		
Requested by: ☐ Phone ☐ Messenger ☐ Mail ☐ Visit	Sent by: ☐ Mail ☐ Visit	☐ Messenger
Searched by	Time Spent	
Date Due	Date Returned	
Refiled by		
Remarks		
Copy 1: Tickler File Copy 3: On Out Card Copy 2: On Record		

Figure 7. Records request.

After the records center staff locates the record and completes all relevant parts of the form, one copy of the form is placed in a "tickler" file under the date when the record is due back in the center. A two- or three-week "checkout" period is common; I prefer two weeks because requesters are less likely to misplace records in the shorter time frame. If the record is not returned by that date, a center staff member calls the user to determine if he or she is done with the record and, if not, to issue an extended due date.

This follow-up procedure is essential if the integrity of the records in the center is to be preserved. Otherwise, many users will forget to return the records when they are done with them. Eventually the records become lost or misplaced.

The second copy of the request form is attached to the record before it is sent to the user. For ease in refiling, this copy stays with the record until it is returned to the center. The third copy of the form is attached to a colored "out" card that replaces the record in its carton. Then if another user requests a checked-out record, tracing it is simple. When the record is returned to the center, you then destroy the second and third copies of the form.

However, the tickler file copies should be refiled by records series title after the record is returned to the center. Then at the end of the year, you can use the tickler forms to manually prepare activity reports on each records series and on the center as a whole.

If the records center index is automated, the tickler file can be kept electronically. Likewise, the activity level of each records series can be compiled by the computer. But unless your company has an electronic mail system, so users can send records requests from their terminals to yours, you'll still need a records request form.

One caution—don't check out entire boxes of records to users. If they must search through a box, have them come to the center work area. If you allow entire boxes to leave the center, you've lost all control over the integrity of the records. It's too easy for users to remove records from the box and forget to return them. Also, when a box is checked out, no one else can use the records from it.

Sometimes even in the best-managed records centers, a record cannot be found. When this situation occurs, return one copy of the form to the requester. In the "remarks" section, explain what steps were taken to search for the record. Keep a second copy of the records request form on file at the records center for use in measuring the center's accuracy at the end of the year. Of course, if the center has an automated indexing system, information on missing records can be stored electronically.

MEASURING THE CENTER'S EFFICIENCY

As an evaluation of the center's efficiency, you should calculate its nonretrieval ratio at least once a year. The formula to use is:

$$\frac{\text{Number of records not found}}{\text{Number of records found}} \times 100 = \underline{\hspace{1cm}}\% \text{ nonretrieval ratio}$$

If the ratio is .5 percent or less, the center is excelling at locating records. If the ratio is over 3 percent, you have a problem.

To determine the cause of the problem, you'll need to analyze some information about the records that were not found. If most of the records not found were requested by a particular department, you'll want to investigate that department's record-keeping practices. Perhaps its records are not complete when they are sent to the center, or perhaps its filing procedures are inaccurate.

If most of the missing records were searched by the same individual in the records center, you may need to work with that person to improve his or her retrieval efforts. And if most of the missing records date back to a time before the center was properly organized, you'll have to decide whether or not it's worth the effort to properly index these older records. (It usually isn't.)

Normally, a high accuracy ratio is due to one of the three problems just outlined. If not, you'll have to play detective until you find a common pattern or link.

STAFFING THE CENTER

In addition to calculating the center's accuracy ratio, you should also do some cost computations. But before we discuss those figures, let's consider one of the major center expenses—the people who operate it.

The size of the center and the amount of activity will determine how heavily you need to staff it. With a small center, you may find the retrieval rate and records volume do not justify keeping the center open all day. If part-time hours seem appropriate, it's better to keep the center open two hours in the morning and two hours in the afternoon than four hours at a stretch. With a "split shift," users don't have to wait unduly long before being able to retrieve records and are, as a result, more receptive to storing their records in the center.

Whatever your center hours are, the odds are that the personnel there will not always be busy with work from the center. Therefore, it's a good idea to have other work available for the slack times, such as preparing documents for microfilming or classifying material that is to be filed.

CENTER COSTS

If you use a commercial center, your costs will be whatever the facility charges you, plus any expenses you may have for transporting the records to and from the center. Usually commercial centers charge a monthly fee for each box stored plus fees for the retrieval and refiling of records and for the adding and removal of boxes. If the center requires you to use its boxes, it will probably charge for the cartons. If you use your own cartons, don't forget to include their cost in your calculations. If all of the center charges do not equal the center's monthly minimum fee, you'll be billed for the minimum instead. (Some centers do not have a minimum fee.)

If you have a company-operated records center, computing its costs will be slightly more involved than for a commercial center. Typical expenses include:

Rent (or if the building is company-owned, depreciation).
Utilities.
Insurance.
Personnel (be sure to include fringe benefits and any temporary help who may be used in peak periods).
Noncapital equipment (equipment that is written off or expensed in the year it is purchased).
Supplies.
Telephone.
Data processing costs (don't forget the programmer's time).
Transportation to and from the center (if it's not located in your building).

Your accounting department should be able to provide you with the appropriate amounts to depreciate and help you prorate rent, utilities, and so on for a center located in a larger building.

Your next step is to total all of the center expenses. Then subtract any revenue the center receives for recycling paper. The figure left is the *net center cost*. Divide this figure by the total holdings in cubic feet for the center's annual *cost per cubic foot*. A standard carton is 1.04 cubic feet; in most cases, you can simply assume each carton is one cubic foot for ease in calculation.

The cost per cubic foot should remain fairly constant. It may even decrease somewhat after the first few years of operation because the capital equipment is fully depreciated and the volume of records in the center has increased.

OTHER CONTROLS

In addition to monitoring the center's accuracy ratio and its cost per cubic foot, you should keep track of the volume of records transferred to the center each year, the volume destroyed, and the volume maintained. As mentioned earlier, a computerized system can generate such reports automatically, but calculating the information manually is not difficult.

If the company is growing, the amount of records kept in the center will grow (even with the most vigorous disposition program). You'll need to monitor that growth and project it into the future, so you'll know ahead of time when the existing center space will be filled and other plans must be made. Also, you'll be better able to project future center personnel needs.

RECORDS DESTRUCTION

An important part of the records center's responsibilities is the destruction of records whose retention period has expired. The first step in the process is determining whether or not the records are confidential. Typically, the department head makes the determination, although at times the legal department may be involved.

RECYCLING RECORDS

In most cases, recycling is the best alternative for all non-confidential records, as well as for the company's other waste paper. Some sorting of the paper into different categories such as computer printout paper is usually required, but requirements vary from recycler to recycler. Training employees to sort paper and separate out nonrecyclable items into different-colored waste bins is a relatively simple matter. Most employees make the extra effort willingly because they appreciate the company's concern for conserving natural resources.

Some companies receive up to $25,000 a year for their recycled paper—which is certainly preferable to paying a disposal service to haul it away. The only time when recycling might not be effective is when the company is not located near any recyclers or when the company has too little waste paper to justify recycling (an unlikely occurrence in the age of paperwork).

In some cities, recycling is also a viable alternative for confidential records. Certain recyclers will pick up the confidential records in their cartons and place them in a trailer that is then sealed—under the observation of a company representative. The records are then delivered directly to a paper mill, where they are immediately repulped. The company receives a letter certifying the destruction, and if desired, the company representative can accompany the records to the paper mill to verify their destruction.

Other Destruction Methods

Probably the most popular method for destroying confidential records is shredding. Not only are shredders clean, efficient, and economical, but a wide range of models are available. Large shredders can handle hundreds of pounds of paper per hour, while smaller models handle just a few pounds.

A ¼ inch shredding width is normally adequate, but for highly confidential material you may wish to use ⅛ inch or even ¹⁄₁₆ inch. The narrower the shred, the lower the capacity and speed at which the shredder can operate. After the paper is shredded, it can be baled or recycled.

Disintegrators are not machines from the latest science fiction movie, but they do carry the shredding concept one step further. These machines chop the records into minute bits, which are then forced through a screen with the aid of a vacuum. The screen insures that no large pieces remain. Destruction is total.

Pulpers are another effective tool for destroying confidential records. The documents are fed into a water-filled tank and "chewed up" in much the same way as in a garbage disposal. The resulting pulp then has its excess moisture removed and, in a semi-dry state, is expelled in a container for hauling away. The water is then recycled for the next batch of records. Pulping machines are easy to operate and can handle large volumes of records efficiently.

So far, we've discussed the most desirable methods for destroying confidential records. Fire or incineration is one of the least satisfactory methods in use. The primary objection is environmental. Unless a very elaborate and expensive incinerator is used, burning records will pollute the atmosphere. For this reason, many communities prohibit such incineration.

Another risk with incineration is that the records will not be completely destroyed. Remember the detective stories where the unburned scrap of paper in the fireplace provides the key clue. In the same way, unless the incineration is very thorough, some records may not be totally destroyed.

Another undesirable method is burying records in a landfill. Not only is the practice environmentally unsound, but the records can even be unearthed.

CHAPTER 6

Vital Records: Your Organization's Lifeblood

In the 1950s and early 1960s, when civil defense was a major national concern, many companies developed elaborate strategies for resuming operations after "the bomb" hit. These civil defense plans included provisions for protecting those records that were considered "vital" or necessary to the organization's survival. Today, however, most people feel—quite understandably—that if a nuclear holocaust were to occur, their only concern would be survival, not reopening a business. One unfortunate result of this belief has been a declining interest in vital records protection.

Of course, it's true that protecting key records from nuclear destruction is probably a futile effort; but still, there are other very important reasons for establishing vital records programs. Fire is the most obvious. We've recently realized that rescuing people from fires in skyscrapers is very difficult; rescuing records is usually out of the question. Losing those records can have a devastating effect on a business. According to a study conducted by the Safe Manufacturers National Association, 43 percent of the businesses that lose their records in a fire either never reopen or fail within six months.

Other very real natural dangers include earthquakes, floods, tornadoes, hurricanes, and even volcanoes. In addition to unavoidable natural calamities, companies are also vulnerable to bombs, other explosive devices, arson, and sabotage by disgruntled employees or angry members of the public.

Consequently, *every* organization—large or small—needs a vital records program to protect essential information from destruction. In fact, small companies can be even more vulnerable than large ones because all of their records and operations are often at one site. Large companies are less vulnerable if duplicate copies of some vital information are kept at more than one site through routine business practices. However, without a vital records program, even the large multilocation firm will not have protected all its key records.

WHAT ARE VITAL RECORDS?

Now that we've established the necessity of a vital records program for all organizations, it's time to define the term "vital records" more precisely. The quick, superficial definition is "those records needed to resume operations in the event of a disaster." That definition includes most but not all vital records. For example, the company's employee pension records aren't necessary to resume its operations, yet they are considered vital because they represent a legal commitment the company has made and must fulfill. So let's expand our definition to also include those records needed to protect:

The rights of employees and customers.
The equity of the business's owners (that is, the stockholders, partners, proprietor, or even the public—in the case of the government).
The organization's legal and financial status.

Now we have a comprehensive general definition of vital records. Each different type of organization has to refine this definition further on the basis of on its own business. For example, a manufacturing company would consider vital those engineering drawings and specifications necessary to produce its products. A hospital's vital records would include its patients' medical files, and a bank's would include the status of each depositor's account.

Although organizations have these unique needs, certain general categories are usually vital. These include records that are necessary to:

Determine receivables (what customers and other groups owe the company).
Determine liabilities (what the company owes to others).

Identify the company's fixed assets (its land, buildings, plants, and equipment) and their value.

Identify the locations and amounts of cash and securities owned by the company.

Identify and, when possible, fulfill existing commitments to customers.

Rebuild facilities (when appropriate).

Develop new business.

State salaries and benefits due employees and former employees (pension, vacation, insurance, and so on).

State any other corporate commitments to employees, such as union contracts.

Meet corporate legal and financial requirements (documents such as the incorporation certificate, the bylaws, and the stock record books).

Resume manufacture of products and identify the nature and value of inventory (for manufacturing firms).

One final major vital records category that overlaps many of those we've already named is those records necessary to resume data processing operations. Computer tapes and disks consolidate large amounts of key information very compactly. Consequently, if key storage media are destroyed, reconstructing the information can be very costly or even impossible. Also, data processing storage media are especially susceptible to damage from adverse environmental conditions.

Many data processing departments have recognized the danger of data loss and have developed their own programs to protect this information. Of course, this simplifies your task, as you have only to incorporate data processing's program into the overall vital records program. However, you cannot automatically assume that the data processing department has adequately protected all vital information. These records must be investigated with as much care as any others.

IDENTIFYING YOUR VITAL RECORDS

Approximately 2 percent of most companies' records can be classified as vital. The question is "Which 2 percent?" Since you cannot proceed until you know what records the organization has, you must first prepare the retention schedule listing all of the organization's records (see Chapter 4). This list is your starting point.

The process is a simple but time-consuming editing of the list. First, all nonessential records (those that do not meet our definition of a vital record) are eliminated. Next, those records that have essential data that can be reconstructed from other records are removed from the list. For example, accounts payable information is kept in several forms—only one would be deemed vital. Finally, those records remaining on the list are reevaluated to insure that they are vital. As a very rough rule of thumb, the longer an organization must keep a record, the more likely that record is vital. So those records with retention values over seven years should be scrutinized very closely.

THE VITAL RECORDS COMMITTEE

While it might seem logical to ask the various department heads to identify which of their records are vital, that idea does not work in practice. Most department heads will declare that virtually all of their records are vital because they view those records as essential to their departments' work—which is not the same as being essential to the company's existence. In fact, no one person has the in-depth knowledge of all key company areas that is necessary to determine which records are vital. Consequently, a top-level vital records committee, using the process outlined above, should select the vital records.

Although the exact membership of the committee will vary from company to company, typically the committee should include:

The records manager.
A corporate lawyer (possibly the general counsel).
The controller or other key finance department member.
An experienced member of the data processing department. (If data processing already has a vital records protection program, your best choice is someone who was instrumental in establishing it.)
The personnel or human resources manager.

Top members of selected key departments such as sales/marketing and operations/production.

The individuals on the committee should (1) be very familiar with their areas and the records in those areas and (2) be willing and able to devote substantial amounts of time to the program until it's operational. While the records manager might seem the logical choice to head the committee, he or she is usually lower on the corporate totem pole than many of the other committee members and may, as a result, have difficulty in obtaining cooperation. The president or CEO (chief executive officer) usually appoints the committee head, and the main requirement, in addition to those already named, is the ability to motivate and work with the other members of the committee.

Usually a good plan is to have the committee schedule regular weekly meetings until all the vital records are identified and adequately protected. And, of course, the president and board of director should approve the entire vital records program before it "becomes law."

Once the program is established, the committee should review the entire schedule annually. And if new records series are added to the retention schedule during the year, the committee should meet then to determine if these records are vital.

PROTECTING YOUR VITAL RECORDS

After the company's vital records are identified, the vital records committee must select an appropriate way to protect these records. Most companies use a combination of strategies, depending on the record and its normal usage patterns. The goal is to use the simplest, most economical method that fits the circumstances. The choices are:

Existing dispersal
Planned dispersal
Protecting the original
Duplicating the record
On-site vaults

Existing dispersal. "Existing dispersal" is the formal title for the vital records protection you already have. As a normal part of doing business, copies of the records are sent to other company locations. For example, both a branch office and the corporate headquarters might have copies of key personnel records for employees at the branch office. However, since the records of corporate headquarters employees would probably not be protected this way, you would need to use another method for them.

As a corollary to existing dispersal within the company, when copies of your company's vital records are kept on file by other groups, those records may—under certain circumstances—be considered protected. The qualifier here is that the outside group's interests are compatible with your company's. For example, considering your creditors' records of the company's liabilities as existing dispersal would be a mistake because their interests are not the same as your company's. On the other hand, data filed with a government agency might be considered protected—if the agency keeps the record for as long as you would need it.

Another problem with depending on outside groups is that they may change their retention standards without your knowledge. Consequently, if you use dispersal to outside groups as protection, you should check their retention practices annually.

Planned dispersal. Another form of protection that makes use of existing copies is planned dispersal. Here one copy of the record is sent off-site to a vital records center after it is no longer needed in the office. As you'll see later in this chapter, a vital records center is not the same as the records center we discussed in Chapter 5. Sending a copy to the vital records center does not eliminate the need to store a copy in the records center for immediate inactive use.

Protecting the original. In cases where the original record is used very infrequently, it may be sent to the vital records center. If necessary, a microfilm copy or other duplicate can be kept on-site for referencing. Minutes of the board of directors' meetings and old ledgers are records whose originals are often protected in this manner.

Duplicating the record. If the options just outlined are not feasible, then a duplicate copy of the record should be made and sent to the vital records center. Microfilm copies are often used to save space and reduce storage expense.

On-site vaults. One other option exists—storing vital records on-site in vaults or safes. Because even the best vaults or safes have their limitations, this option should be reserved for short-term storage of vital records that are updated or changed frequently. In these circumstances, copies should still be sent off-site on a regular basis for maximum protection of the information.

Because vaults and safes are extremely heavy, they must be placed in a portion of the building that is structurally able to support them. Such equipment should meet the specifications and requirements of three groups: Underwriters Laboratories (UL), the National Fire Protection Association, and the Safe Manufacturers National Association.

Ironically, many organizations have excellent vaults but use them to store nonvital records. Or they may even treat the vault as a giant closet complete with inflammable cleaning materials. The vault may also be left open and unattended. Imagine how you'd feel if anyone could stroll into your bank's vault and look around. Vaults are major investments; they should be used properly.

A somewhat less expensive variant of the vault is the insulated or fire-resistant file cabinet. Such files are expensive and heavy (almost 500 pounds for an empty four-drawer letter-size vertical file). While these files reduce the chance of records' being destroyed by fire, they do not provide adequate overall protection for your vital records. They are most effectively used for records whose information could be reconstructed but only through substantial expenditures of time or money. As with safes and vaults, these files should be tested by Underwriters Laboratories. Also, you must be sure the building is structurally able to tolerate the weight.

THE VITAL RECORDS CENTER

Throughout this chapter, we've mentioned the vital records center. This is an off-site facility specially designed for the protection of key records. While a few very large corporations have found it practical to build their own vital records centers, most companies find it more economical to rent space in a commercial vital records facility.

Commercial vital records centers are somewhat different from the commercial records centers we discussed in Chapter 5, although some centers provide both services. Vital records centers are usually located in relatively unpopulated areas, unlikely to be attacked in a war.

The centers are often underground and take advantage of previous natural or man-made excavations. Not only is underground storage extremely secure, but it also provides a naturally controlled temperature and humidity. For example, Underground Vaults and Storage, Inc. of Hutchinson, Kansas, is located in a working salt mine; while Iron Mountain Security Storage Corp., Hudson, New York, is in an iron mine. Southern Vital Records in Flora, Mississippi, is located in a former munitions bunker; and Perpetual Storage, Inc., which was built as a vault, was hollowed out of a granite mountain in Utah.

Vital records centers typically have security safeguards reminiscent of James Bond novels. They also have their own internal firefighting systems and are not normally dependent on the public water supply. (Water mains could break in a disaster.) Not surprisingly, your records are most vulnerable while they are in transit to the vital records center. Consequently, duplicate or backup copies should be kept until the records arrive safely at the center.

Some vital records centers accept only computer tapes and microfilm, while other also accept paper records. Storage charges at a vital records center are usually on a "per tape" or "per carton" basis with a minimum annual fee. Companies with large amounts of vital records can rent rooms or vaults at the vital records center.

THE VITAL RECORDS SCHEDULE

A key aspect of the vital records program is the preparation of a comprehensive vital records schedule. Like the records disposition schedule, the vital records listing will form an important part of the records manual (see Chapter 11). Figure 8 shows a typical format for a vital records schedule.

The "records series title" is, of course, the official one, whereas "media" indicates whether the record is kept on paper, microfilm, magnetic tape, and so on. "Method of protection" explains whether the record is protected by existing dispersal or stored in a vital records center or on-site vault. This column should also indicate which copy of the record is being protected. "Frequency of deposit" indicates how often a changing record is sent off-site: daily, weekly,

VITAL RECORDS SCHEDULE				Date	Page
Records Series Title	Media	Method of Protection		Frequency of Deposit	Retention

Figure 8. Vital records schedule.

monthly, and so on. "Retention" is listed here because the record might not be classified "vital" for its entire life span, and as a result, the retention schedule value might not be appropriate here.

Since this schedule will be much shorter than the retention schedule, the records can usually be listed alphabetically by title. Just as with the retention listing, the vital records schedule should be reviewed annually and new records added as needed. And as you might expect, the entire records manual, including these schedules, is itself a vital record.

TESTING THE VITAL RECORDS PROGRAM

Just as your company holds (or should hold) periodic fire drills, so should it also test the vital records program to insure that it will function properly if a disaster occurs. The first step in the test is picking a team of employees who would have to reconstruct operations in the event of a disaster. The employees are then given a set of information needs the organization would have after the disaster. Using only the records protected in the vital records program, the employees must demonstrate that they can recreate the data and provide the appropriate information.

Here are some sample test problems:

Continue paying employees on time and making all proper payroll deductions.

Prepare a current inventory of all company assets.

Send revised shipping instructions to vendors with outstanding orders.

Prepare an insurance claim for a portion of the facility.

Collect all information needed to resume manufacture of a particular product or to resume service in a certain area.

Regular tests with varying problems help measure the system's continuing effectiveness and keep employees alert and prepared to cope with a crisis. The tests also increase awareness of the vital records program and its importance.

CHAPTER 7

Managing the Organization's Files

Up to now, we've dealt primarily with inactive records. For many organizations, that's where their records management program stops. Individual departments are allowed to maintain their active working records any way they wish. This system can create substantial problems. Secretaries often develop filing systems they alone understand, so problems arise when they're absent. Several departments may keep unnecessary and costly duplicate files instead of sharing one common set of information. The wrong types of filing equipment may be selected, thus slowing retrieval and wasting both space and money. And finally, when the records go to inactive storage, they may be in an order intelligible only to the original filer—thus complicating retrieval.

All of these problems stem from the fact that most departments (1) do not have the expertise to establish the most effective filing systems and (2) do not regard filing as a priority—at least, not until they can't find a record. Hence, it makes sense to involve professionals—the records management staff in departmental filing systems. However, before we discuss the records manager's various options in establishing and maintaining active files, we need to examine the choices available—both in filing systems and in filing equipment.

FILING SYSTEMS

No one type of filing system should be adopted for all records series. Instead, the records manager should use a variety of systems, depending on the type of material to be filed and the ways that the material will need to be retrieved. Another important consideration is ease in separating out records for destruction or inactive storage. Keeping these criteria in mind, let's examine the various types of filing systems. Such systems fall into three categories: alphabetic, numeric, and alphanumeric.

Alphabetic Filing by Name

Filing material alphabetically by name is the oldest, simplest, and most commonly used of all filing systems. Typical applications include personnel files, vendor files, and customer files. The system's primary virtue is its simplicity. No index is needed to find a particular file, and classifying the material to be filed is relatively straightforward.

However, even the simplest system has drawbacks. In an alphabetic system of over 10,000 files, confusion over a name's proper spelling can make retrieval difficult. The name "Burke," for example, can also be spelled Berk, Berke, Birk, Birke, and Burk. In a small system, finding the correct spelling is relatively easy, but in a large system, searching is time-consuming, costly, and frustrating. Also, for a large system, typing the complete names on file folder labels involves a substantial amount of time, unless the labels are prepared automatically by a computer or word processor.

The other potential problem with alphabetic filing is errors due to unclear or nonexistent filing rules. For example, does "Mac-Dougal" go before or after "McDonald"?* And does "WGN Television" go at the beginning of the *W*s or after "Weldo Repairs, Inc." and before "Wimbley Widget Co."?** Some organizations solve these problems by developing their own set of standardized filing rules to cover such situations. However, a simpler, more effective solution is to adopt ARMA's *Rules for Alphabetical Filing* as the company standard in this area. Copies of the rules can be obtained from ARMA for a nominal charge. Their adoption helps insure standard alphabetic filing practices throughout the company. And since the same rules are included in many secretarial textbooks, they are gaining broad acceptance.

*Answer: before, unless there are enough entries under *Mac* and *Mc* to justify treating them as a separate section before the other *M*s.
**Answer: at the beginning of the *W*s.

Geographic filing. Geographic filing is a specialized variation of alphabetic filing. This system is used for documents whose primary reference is location, such as maps, real estate materials, and information on various cities' industrial development programs. The file is usually subdivided into a geographic hierarchy, with each level alphabetized. For example, information might first be grouped by county or state, with these filed in alphabetic order. Then files on various cities in a particular county or state would be filed alphabetically behind that county or state. So under "Texas," we might have general information on the state followed by files on Austin, Dallas, and so on.

Numeric Filing Systems

With the exception of chronological files, numeric filing systems are characterized by (1) the use of a unique number to identify a particular document or file and (2) the need for an index to cross-reference the number with what it represents. The other three numeric filing systems are: consecutive, terminal-digit, and middle-digit.

Consecutive numeric filing. Consecutive numeric filing is the simplest of the numeric systems. As the name implies, documents or files are placed in consecutive order according to their assigned numbers. This system is commonly used for purchase orders, checks, bills of lading, invoices, print shop order files, and similar types of records that have unique numbers randomly assigned to each document or file.

Consecutive numeric systems work very well for files of up to 10,000 records. At that point, three problems arise. First, it is more time-consuming to file documents with five-digit numbers. Second, the likelihood of error is substantially greater when five digits are filed consecutively instead of four. Third, since the most recently created documents are the most frequently referenced, filing activity is greatest at the end of the numeric series. Typically, you will have several files personnel working in the same area and getting in each other's way.

Terminal-digit filing. Terminal-digit filing, a numeric system for files with over 10,000 folders, was developed to eliminate the problems of consecutive numeric filing. For example, universities typically assign students "numbers" to avoid confusion if there are two "John Smiths." Yet if a university with 40,000 students, each with a 9-digit student number, tried to file consecutively, the problems just described would be mind-boggling. To avoid these difficulties, the terminal-digit system is based on the principle of filing "backward" in groups of two or three digits. The example below demonstrates how the system works by showing the same numbers filed consecutively and by the terminal-digit method.

Numeric Files In Consecutive Order	The Same Numeric Files in a Terminal-Digit Sequence		
	First	Middle	Terminal
10022	11	03	19
10023	5	18	20
50123	1	00	22
51820	18	00	22
61822	29	01	22
110319	6	18	22
180022	1	00	23
290122	5	01	23

With the terminal-digit method, all files ending in 00 would be grouped together first, then those ending in 01, and so on. With the files in the example, all of those ending in 19 came before those ending in 20 and so on. Next the files are grouped by their middle digits so that the 00 22s come before the 01 22s. And finally, the files are ordered by their first digits, so 1 00 22 precedes 18 or 22. As you'll also note, files which would be next to each other in a consecutive system such as 10022 and 10023 are now separated. If necessary, the system can use groups of three digits, instead of one or two, for the first and middle groupings.

Although this system may initially sound confusing, once filing personnel are trained, fewer misfiles occur. Errors decrease because files personnel are working with groups of one, two, or three digits instead of a long string of five or more digits. Terminal-digit filing works well with color-coded systems (discussed later in this chapter). Such systems further reduce misfiles.

The other main advantage to terminal-digit systems is that the newest and presumably most heavily referenced files are "spread out" through the cabinets instead of concentrated at the end, as happens with consecutive numeric files. Consequently, files personnel work uniformly throughout the system, and "traffic jams" are avoided.

Terminal-digit filing is frequently used for large, active numeric files such as hospital patient records and insurance policy files. Today, many such large files are automated or stored on microfiche, often with computer-assisted retrieval. Some of the fiche systems do use terminal-digit systems and modifications thereof. And when paper records are still the most cost-effective option, terminal-digit filing is a highly effective system.

Middle-digit filing. One of terminal-digit filing's advantages can also be a disadvantage. Namely, if you want to retrieve 100 consecutively numbered files, you must go to 100 different locations in the filing system. Middle-digit filing was designed to eliminate that problem and is used for the same types of files as terminal digit systems are.

Just as the names implies, filing begins with the middle digits. Then the records are filed by the first digits and finally by the terminal digits. Consequently, as the example below shows, files whose middle digits are 00 would be first, then 01, and so on.

Numeric Files in Consecutive Order	The Same Numeric Files in a Middle-Digit Sequence		
	First	Middle	Terminal
10022	1	00	22
10023	1	00	23
50120	12	00	01
60119	5	01	20
60120	6	01	19
120001	6	01	20
160101	16	01	01

Because 100 consecutive files, such as 1 00 00 to 1 00 99, are located together, it is easier to convert a consecutive numeric system to middle-digit filing than to terminal-digit. When supplemented by color-coded systems, middle-digit, like terminal-digit, has a low frequency of errors. Middle-digit's one possible disadvantage is that filing activity will be concentrated in the 100 folder groups of newer records. Also, it may take personnel slightly longer to adjust to a middle-digit system than to a terminal-digit system because the numeric ordering is somewhat more complex.

Chronological filing systems. One other type of numeric filing system deserves a brief mention. Chronological filing (filing by date) is appropriate when the date is the primary means of reference for a document. Computer printouts and "tickler files" are typical examples of chronological files. Chronological filing is frequently used in combination with other filing systems. Thus, documents are placed in file folders chronologically. Also, new files may be established each year for a particular records series, with the preceding year's records going to the records center.

Subject Files

Subject files can fall into either the alphabetic or alphanumeric category. In a small system, such as an executive's correspondence files, the various subjects are often filed alphabetically. For larger systems, such as departmental or companywide subject files, alphanumeric codes may be assigned to each main subject and its subdivisions. Such codes have one or more letters indicating the overall subject, such as "Budgets," followed by a series of numbers for each subdivision. B2-1, for example, might be "Budgets, Monthly—Variance Reports."

Subject filing is often used for correspondence and general administrative files. However, its most important use is the uniform filing system—a master plan for organizing all of the organization's records by subject. Later in this chapter, we'll discuss uniform filing systems in depth.

With subject filing, the main difficulty is classification. Deciding where to file a document and where and when to cross-reference it requires careful thought, as opposed to alphabetic and numeric filing, where filing decisions are obvious. To simplify the process, all subjects should be clearly defined in writing, and this information should be given to filing personnel. It's also a good idea, when possible, to use senior files personnel for subject filing. And of course, they should be trained thoroughly and their work checked until they demonstrate a mastery of the system.

Phonetic Filing Systems

Phonetic filing systems are designed to cope with the problems of finding names in a large alphabetic file (over 10,000 names) when you're unsure of the proper spelling. Soundex, one of the most popular phonetic systems, assigns an alphanumeric code to each name based on consonant sounds. All names that sound similar have the same code. Thus, all the Burkes, Birkes, Berkes, Burks, and so forth would have the same code (B-620 in Soundex), followed by the appropriate first name, which can also be coded. The "6" represents the R-sound and the "2" the K. Since all Soundex codes must have three digits, a "0" is assigned at the end as a "placeholder." The listing would be:

B-620 Albert
B-620 Alicia
B-620 Allan

and so on, regardless of the spelling of Burke.

The complete Soundex coding rules are too elaborate to detail here. However, after the initial letter of the surname and a dash, the numbers 1–6 are assigned to consonant sounds as follows:

1   B, F, P, V
2   C, G, J, K, Q, S, X, Z
3   D, T
4   L
5   M,N
6   R

H and *W* are regarded as nonexistent. Thus Adams is A-352, Brown is B-650, and Shaw is Shaw-000 (no codable consonants).

Soundex and other similar systems are primarily used in large government files. For example, one state uses a computerized Soundex system to match current and previous reports of child abuses, while another state uses it for files of individuals with criminal records. Soundex excels in these applications because the proper spelling of a last name is often unknown.

Because of the complexity of the coding rules and the difficulty of detecting a coding error once it is made, automating the coding and searching processes is highly desirable.

The filing systems just described provide you with an extensive array of options. Remember to choose the best system for each records series on an individual basis rather than making all or most records series conform to one option.

Filing Equipment

Your choices in filing equipment are even more extensive than in filing systems. Once again, you'll need to determine the particular needs of each department and the specifications of each records series; then select the equipment that best meets those requirements. For filing equipment decisions, the primary concerns are:

Access frequency. How frequently will material in the files be used? If demands are heavy and more than one person may retrieve records, you'll want a system where all records are physically available at the same time.

Retrieval speed. How quickly must the material be found? Must it, for example, be retrieved during a phone conversation?

Filing features. What size and type are the records—legal-size folders, letter-size folders, card files, computer printouts? Does the entire file folder need to be pulled or just selected items from it?

Space requirements. Must the equipment fit in a particular sized area? Is a limited amount of space available?

Space cost versus equipment cost. If you're located in a "high-rent district," expensive equipment that can hold a large amount of records in a small space may be cost-justified.

Structural considerations. All types of filing equipment are heavy—some more so than others. Consequently, you'll need to consider the stress the *filled* equipment will place on the building.

Security requirements. How confidential are the records? Filing equipment with locks is expensive and only provides "controlled access" because the locks can be opened easily with a "master key," hairpin, or other device. All the locks do is prevent passers-by from opening the files. Anyone who really wants to open the cabinets will be able to. If files are to be really secure, they should be kept in a room that can be locked and that has a person guarding the entrance when it is unlocked.

Fire protection. The different types of filing equipment provide varying levels of fire protection. So you should determine what problems would arise if the records were destroyed by fire and protect them accordingly, either by special equipment or by off-site storage of duplicate copies.

Mobility. Is the company planning to move to another location? Are people (and their records) frequently moved within the building? If so, you'll need filing equipment that can be moved easily.

Growth of the files. You should consider how rapidly the files will grow and what your future needs are before committing to a system.

Now let's see how well the various types of filing equipment meet these criteria.

Vertical Files

The vertical file cabinet (see Figure 9) is the oldest of the filing equipment options. In recent years, it's been maligned, primarily

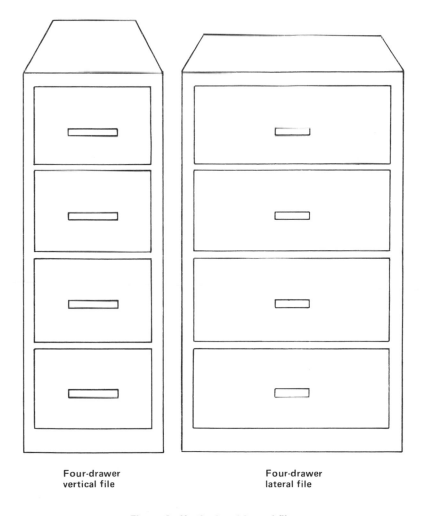

Four-drawer
vertical file

Four-drawer
lateral file

Figure 9. Vertical and lateral files.

because it's been misused. The vertical file is still a good choice for storing records in individual offices or small departments. However, if more than four vertical file cabinets are needed in an area, you should consider other options, because at that point vertical files no longer use space efficiently.

If you are going to use vertical files, allow 44 inches of aisle space in front of the cabinets for pulling out drawers and retrieving records. Five-drawer vertical files are normally preferable to four-drawer because you get an additional drawer's storage for relatively little extra expense and no extra floor space. However, some people have difficulty seeing into the top drawer. Consequently, the primary users' heights must be considered.

For safety reasons, vertical files should be bolted either to the walls or to each other. Otherwise, there is a real danger of a file's tipping over if a user has two drawers open at once.

Since a drawer must be opened before a record can be found, retrieval and filing are relatively slow. Also, only one person can use a file cabinet at a time. However, a retrieval/filing advantage is that documents can be added to or removed from a folder without the user's first removing the entire folder.

Vertical files are less expensive than lateral files for individual office records. They're also relatively easy to move and can be moved while full. With locks, they provide controlled access.

However, for large records series, vertical files are more expensive than open-shelf files and waste space. Also, they provide no real fire protection unless they are specially insulated. Although the cabinet does not burn because it is metal, it conducts heat extremely well. As a result, in a fire, the cabinet becomes an oven and "cooks" your records.

Lateral Files

Lateral files (also shown in Figure 9) are the interior decorator's dream—an attractive file cabinet. As the name "lateral" implies, folders are filed sideways, not front to back as in a vertical cabinet. As a result, the cabinets use more wall space, but do not extend out into the room as far.

Lateral cabinets fall into two categories: those with pull-out drawers and those with doors that slide into the cabinet revealing shelves for filing. Records in both types are typically filed left to right. The drawer style, however, can be adapted with dividers so that documents may be filed front to back as in a vertical file. Lateral files with drawers require 30 inches of aisle space, and those with doors a few inches less.

Lateral cabinets are excellent for personal files and small records series in "open plan" office areas. In these landscaped work areas, appearance is important, and the lateral file can serve as a "wall" or divider between work areas. However, these benefits have a price: Lateral files cost substantially more than vertical ones.

Just as with vertical cabinets, the higher the lateral file, the more efficiently it uses space. However, the five-drawer lateral model may be difficult for shorter personnel to use. Models with doors and shelf filing don't present this problem, since you don't look down into the shelf as you do with a drawer.

Retrieval is not particularly fast because drawers and doors must be opened and closed. Of course, the doors can be left open, but in that case, open-shelf files (our next option) would be a more economical alternative. And with the drawers, only one person can work in a cabinet at a time.

Lateral files are relatively easy to move, although the drawers normally have to be emptied. With locks, the cabinets provide good controlled access. And when documents are filed left to right, lateral files provide slightly better fire protection than vertical cabinets. However, for any real fire protection, you'll need insulated fire-resistant lateral files.

Open-Shelf Filing

Open-shelf files (see Figure 10) are an often-overlooked, economical alternative for departmental and other medium-size to large filing systems. As the name implies, open-shelf files hold files sideways, just as a lateral file does, but without any doors. Open-shelf units may be six, seven, or eight shelves high. Because there are no pullout drawers, the height presents no retrieval problems. In terms of cost per filing inch, open-shelf units are the cheapest of all filing equipment. They are also one of the most space-efficient options.

Open-shelf units provide fast retrieval, as there are no doors or drawers to be opened. And several individuals can retrieve files simultaneously. When used in combination with a color-coded

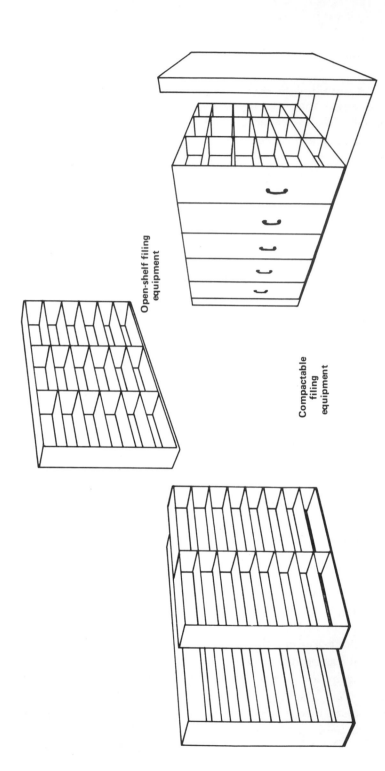

Open-shelf filing equipment

Compactable filing equipment

Figure 10. Open-shelf and compactable filing equipment.

filing system, the open-shelf units reduce misfiles because visual checks instantly reveal any major filing errors.

Given all these virtues, you may be wondering why open-shelf files are not more prevalent. One reason is the misconception that they're ugly; massive olive green units spring to mind. Today, however, open-shelf units are available in the same wide range of colors as lateral files. And when the open-shelf unit is combined with a color-coded filing system, the end result is both attractive and practical. Another reason open-shelf filing is not more common is that some vendors do not promote the systems heavily because they are less expensive than other options.

Of course, open-shelf units do have their disadvantages. The units are more difficult to move than vertical or lateral files because they must be emptied and may need to be disassembled. Also, there is no controlled access. If the files are unattended, any passer-by can quickly find and remove a folder. In the event of a fire, the records are extremely susceptible to water damage, and the front sides in particular are vulnerable to the flames.

Compactable Files

Compactable files (also shown in Figure 10) are a variation of open-shelf filing designed for use in situations where space is at a premium. The open-shelf files are mounted on tracks imbedded in the floor. The filing units slide along the tracks so users can get to the records they need. Consequently, all records are not available at the same time.

Both automated and manual compactable file systems are available. For small systems (five or six units), the less expensive manual units are quite effective. No real physical strength is required to maneuver the manual units, and you don't have to worry about breakdowns. With the automated version, the user simply presses a button, and the files open at the appropriate aisle. When the files are automated, it's usually a good idea to purchase a maintenance contract to insure prompt service in case of a breakdown.

Both types of compactable files require building alterations (that is, installing the tracks). Consequently, moving the units to another location is a major operation, which may require the vendor's assistance. Also, because the files themselves are heavy and consolidate a great many records in a very small space, they place additional stress on the building and must be located accordingly.

Compactable files are ideal for situations where current office space is limited and where acquiring additional space would be costly. For example, one company I worked with had "outgrown" its building and was renting additional space in the surrounding area. Converting to open plan offices and installing manual compactable filing systems enabled them to bring several departments back into the building. For this company, cost-justifying the new filing equipment was easy. Compactable files are especially appropriate for "high-rent districts" like New York City, Chicago, and San Francisco, where office space may cost $40 or more a square foot.

Compactable files do slow retrieval, as users must open the appropriate aisle before pulling a record. Also, depending on which aisle is open, other users may have to wait to retrieve a record. Obviously, records in open units are quite vulnerable to fire and water damage. And there is no controlled access except for automated units when the power is turned off.

Automated Files

Automated or motorized files (also known as "power files") are the Rolls Royce of filing equipment. These files bring the record to the user instead of the user's going to the record. Although the interior construction of these units varies, they basically operate in the same way. The files are stored on shelves in the large, enclosed metal unit, which looks like a huge box. The operator sits before the unit and presses a button to indicate the appropriate shelf. The shelf is then automatically moved into position in front of the operator for retrieval.

Automated files are extremely expensive in terms of cost, installation, and maintenance. A service contract is needed, and if the company is not located in a major metropolitan area, repairs can be a problem. Some units do have a system for manual operation if the equipment breaks down; this feature is an advantage, as otherwise the files are virtually inaccessible until repairs are made. However, manual operation is slow and cumbersome. One organization in Wyoming practically had a mutiny of files personnel after two weeks of hand-cranking the files while waiting for the repairperson.

Automated units are extremely heavy. Consequently, the stress placed on the building must be considered. Also, these units require building modifications and, along with compactable files, are the most difficult system to move.

Automated files do provide fast access with a minimum of operator effort. (Of course, only one person can use a unit at a time.) And the units store large amounts of records in a small amount of space.

But quite frankly, the only applications I recommend them for are storage of large card files (pharmacy prescriptions, for example) and microfiche or -film. For paper records storage, the automated files are a dinosaur. The money spent on the files could be better used converting the paper records to microfilm or -fiche. Automated files provide a short-term solution for paper records. As more records accumulate, more units must be purchased. The files are a quick fix, not a lasting solution.

COLOR-CODING YOUR FILES

Color-coding is a relatively inexpensive adjunct to your filing systems and equipment. Color-coding speeds the retrieval and refiling of records while reducing misfiles. As an added benefit, it can brighten the entire office environment when used in an open-shelf filing system.

With a straight numeric, middle-digit, or terminal-digit filing system, a different color can be used with each digit from 0 to 9. This sytem creates bands of colors in the files and makes it easy to spot out-of-place folders. Thus, in a terminal-digit system, if 1 is red and 7 blue, all files with numbers ending in 17 would form a red and blue band. Usually the color-coding is extended on through the system up to, but not including, the last filing digit. To carry our example further, the numbers 10 89 17 and 11 89 17 would have five identical colors. The italicized digits—the last filing digits in a terminal-digit system—would be uncolored. With this system, simply by matching colors, a folder would always be within nine folders of its correct place.

A similar approach can be used for alphabetic and alphanumeric systems, with a different color assigned to each letter. A wide range of color-coded systems are available from vendors. You should choose a system that has strong, easily differentiated colors to minimize filing errors.

Color can also be used to differentiate dates. Thus, the 1981 files might have yellow labels, the 1982 orange, and so on. This insures that a 1981 file doesn't accidentally get placed in the 1982 section.

Another use of color in filing systems is colored file folders. For example, red folders can be used for confidential or limited-access files. Colored folders can also be used to designate files belonging to different departments, such as blue for marketing, yellow for accounting, and so on. However, since the colored folders are usually quite a bit more expensive than their plain manila counterparts, be sure you have a good reason for using them.

Still another effective use of color is for "out cards." Either all of the out cards can be one color, or cards of different colors can be used for different departments. In either case, the name of the person who has the record and the removal date should be written on the card itself or on a charge-out slip, which is inserted in a pocket on the card. The cards with pockets are preferable, as a second copy of the charge-out slip can be placed in a tickler file. This system makes it easy for files personnel to check on unreturned records. But whatever the system, out cards are a "must" for all records except those in an individual's desk or private files. Without out cards, records can easily be lost or misplaced.

Similarly, you can use colored cards to check on filing trainees. Simply have the trainee place a colored card behind each document filed. Then it's a simple process to check the trainee's accuracy, discuss any errors, and remove the cards. Of course, you should use cards of a different color from the out cards to avoid confusion.

However you elect to use color in your files, keep the system(s) simple and easy to remember. Use distinctive colors that stand out clearly. And remember, color does not eliminate the need for a logical filing system, but it does support and enhance the system.

CENTRALIZED FILES—THE OPTIONS

So far, we've discussed the fundamentals of filing systems and equipment—principles that can be applied either to an individual department's files or to a corporate central files department. Now we need to consider whether or not the organization's active files should be combined in one location and what type of overall control should be applied.

You have three basic options. They are:

Central files. All of the organization's active records are controlled by the records management staff and kept in one or more central files areas.

Decentralized files. Each department keeps its own active records and retains full control over them.

Controlled decentralized files. Each department keeps its own files. However, the files are maintained in accordance with the standards set by the records management department and are audited regularly to insure compliance.

Let's examine each of these options separately.

Central Files

With a central files program, all active files except those being created or used at that time are kept in one or more central files rooms. These rooms function as libraries, with records being checked out to users and follow-ups being conducted if the records are not returned on time.

The advantages to central files are:

Fewer misfiles and missing records, because all filing is done by professionals whose sole job is central files.

Elimination of needless storage of duplicate copies.

More efficient use of filing space and equipment.

Better compliance with the retention/disposition program, because the central files staff insures that records are sent to the records center on schedule.

A thorough knowledge and consequently a more effective use of the information kept within the organization.

However, in spite of its advantages, central files is a rather difficult concept to introduce, because most users want *their* records at *their* fingertips. The following guidelines will reduce user resistance and help insure the program's success:

1. *The central files area(s) should be conveniently located for users.* If people have to walk half a mile or go down five floors to retrieve

their records, they're going to be reluctant to send their files to a central location. For this reason, the central files concept is most common in small organizations that are located on two or three floors in a large building or in one small building. Large organizations either set up central files areas in a number of locations or use a more decentralized approach.

2. *The central files concept is most readily accepted in organizations that already have successful records management programs in other areas.* For example, if users have confidence in the records center for storing inactive records, they are more likely to trust their active records to central files. Likewise, the program needs strong upper management support. At one company, the CEO asked that his files be inventoried and incorporated into the central files system first. Of course, other managers were quick to follow his example.

3. *Establish the program gradually.* Bring one department's records into the files area at a time. Otherwise, you'll have confusion and frustrated users.

4. *Do not allow users to retrieve or refile records.* Central files personnel must handle these duties if the integrity of the files is to be preserved and misfiles are to be kept to a minimum. Many organizations use a divided, or Dutch, door to prevent unauthorized personnel from entering the files area.

5. *Ideally, the central files area should open an hour before normal working hours and close an hour later.* It's very frustrating to the employee who's working overtime if needed records are unavailable because the file room is closed. And whatever hours you choose, be sure they're well publicized.

6. *Be sure confidential records are adequately protected.* Many organizations omit legal and personnel records from the central files program for this very reason. Other companies segregate certain records and limit access to them.

7. *Consider using the central files concept selectively.* That is, files that are referenced by several departments, such as hospital patient records and insurance policyholder files, are kept in a central area. Records primarily of interest to one department are maintained in that department.

The above guidelines apply to the central files of today—paper or microfilm records. One other option is now available, but at a premium price. This option is electronic central files. The records (either hard copy or computer/electronic mail-generated) are microfilmed upon their arrival at central files. When a record is needed, the user calls it up on his or her computer terminal. The computer then locates the record. Next, the filmed data is converted to electronic impulses and relayed to the user's terminal. The user either reads the copy on the terminal screen or has a hard copy printed. This system provides speedy retrieval and eliminates the need for the central files area to be physically close to the user. Confidentiality can be insured by having the user's sign-on code indicate what records he or she can have access to.

Decentralized Files

The opposite of central files is, of course, decentralization, with each department controlling and keeping its own records. This is the least desirable option because:

Storage of duplicate copies abounds, and filing space and equipment are used inefficiently.

There is no control over a department's filing practices and systems. Since filing is a low-priority item for many clerical personnel, files are often poorly organized or incomplete, and material to be filed often accumulates. After the records are sent to inactive storage, records center personnel often have difficulty locating a specific record in a carton because of inconsistent filing systems.

Retention policies are less likely to be followed.

While some departments do a good job of managing their records, all too many do not. And that's not surprising; most departmental personnel have not been trained in records management.

Controlled Decentralized Files—The Compromise

For many companies, a controlled decentralized system represents the ideal compromise between central files and decentralization. For other firms, the system serves as a stepping-stone on the way to central files.

With a controlled decentralized system, each department keeps and maintains its own active records. But the records management staff reviews the department's filing systems to insure consistency throughout the organization. For example, all departments would use standard alphabetic filing rules such as those prepared by ARMA. The records management group also trains the department personnel who will classify and file the materials.

The records management staff would also use its broad-based knowledge of the organization's records to increase efficiency further. For example, they might assist two departments located near each other to set up a shared filing system for those records series needed by both.

A UNIFORM FILING SYSTEM

Uniform filing systems take the idea of centralization one step further by superimposing a "master" subject filing system on all of the company's records. A uniform filing system is virtually a "must" with central files, because it greatly simplifies retrieval, groups related records together, and eliminates the accidental storage of duplicate records.

Uniform filing systems can also be used effectively with a controlled decentralized program. In this case, each department classifies and maintains its records according to the uniform system, thus saving the time normally spent in designing its own system. And if the company decides later to convert to central files, the process will be much simpler if the uniform system is already in use.

Developing a Uniform System

Unfortunately, you can't buy a standard uniform filing system and simply impose it on your records. Because different organizations have different types of records, the subject categories for classifying those records also vary. As a result, you'll need to develop a system unique to your organization.

The first step, of course, is obtaining management approval. As with earlier records management projects, publicize this support through a letter from the president or other top executive.

Next, use the data from the records inventory and the retention (disposition) schedule to select major subject headings for the system. Choose appropriate alpha codes for each heading. Alpha codes are desirable because, unlike numeric codes, they instantly remind the users of the subject they represent. Some typical main headings and codes are:

ADM   Administration
ENG   Engineering
FAC   Facilities and equipment
FIN   Finance and accounting
LEG   Legal
MFG   Manufacturing
MKT   Marketing
PER   Personnel
PRD   Production
PUB   Public relations
PUR   Purchasing
SEC   Security

These headings do not refer specifically to the records of various departments but rather to all corporate records pertaining to that subject. For example, the finance department will have records on its employees that fall under the personnel category, while the personnel department's budget records would belong in the finance category. Avoid subject headings such as "forms," "correspondence," and "reports," which indicate the format of the information rather than its contents.

Each subject heading and subheading should have a clear written definition, such as, "Personnel: Information related to (1) the recruitment and hiring of employees and (2) their careers at the company, including appraisals, promotions, salaries, and benefits."

Next, develop major categories or subheadings for each main heading. For example, the personnel category might be broken down as follows:

PER 1   Employment information
PER 2   Wages and salaries
PER 3   Benefits
PER 4   Attendance
and so on . . .

Then each of these categories is divided one more time. For example, PER 3 (Benefits) might be subdivided as follows:

PER 3-1   Health insurance
PER 3-2   Life insurance
PER 3-3   Dental insurance

PER 3-4   Disability insurance
PER 3-5   Pension plan
PER 3-6   Vacations
and so on . . .

The fourth breakdown (PER 3-1-1, for example) is made as needed by either the central files group of the individual departments with the approval of the records manager. Although the uniform filing system is subject-oriented, both alphabetic and numeric filing systems are used in conjunction with it. For example, under the heading "health insurance," the personnel department might have an alphabetic file by employee name.

For easy retrieval, the uniform filing system must be supported by a detailed alphabetic index similar to this sample:

A

Absence, employee	PER 4
Absence, leaves of	PER 4-3
Absence, due to illness	PER 4-2
Acceptance of shipments	PUR 4-1
Accidents	SEC 2
Accidents, automobile	SEC 2-1
Accidents, office	SEC 2-2
and so on . . .	

To develop a successful uniform filing system, you'll need to involve the system's users in the development of the subject headings. Your records coordinators will be particularly helpful here. You'll also need to prepare a filing section for the records manual. This section will include a complete description of the system and instructions on how to implement it. (See Chapter 11 for a detailed discussion of the records manual.) And of course, all filing personnel will need to be trained in the system and supervised during the conversion.

Establishing a uniform filing system is a lot of work, but it's a one-shot effort, just like doing the records inventory. Once the initial effort is over, the company will reap the benefits for years with minimal follow-up. Of course, new subjects will be added to the system as needed, just as new records series are added to the disposition (retention) schedule.

THE FILES AUDIT

To insure that the uniform filing system is being used correctly, the files should be audited regularly, usually once a year. In fact, the files audit should be a part of any controlled decentralized filing program, whether or not a uniform system is in place.

Although the records management department can conduct the audit, it's usually more efficient to have the internal audit department do it as part of its standard operational auditing procedure. This practice has several advantages, the most important being that the internal audit team has "clout." Department heads know that they must comply with its findings. Also, you incur less user resentment if your group does not actually perform the audit. Plus, the records management team has enough to do without conducting audits. If, however, there is no internal audit department, the responsibility is yours.

No matter who conducts the audit, it's the records management department's responsibility to set the standards. Typically, these include:

Legible, accurate labels on all file drawers (or folders in an open-shelf system).

No overcrowding (drawers and shelves have at least three inches of free space).

Use of out cards (if you don't see any, there's a problem).

Use of a tickler file or other follow-up system for records that are checked out.

Conformity with the uniform filing system, if one exists.

Conformity with ARMA rules for alphabetic filing.

Existence of an up-to-date index where appropriate (for numeric files, for example).

Conformity with the records disposition or retention schedule.

The auditors should also interview both files personnel and users to find out if any problems exist or if either group has any suggestions for improving the system.

A files audit is not a "trap" to get people in trouble; instead, it's a control device. For it to be a success, departments should know in advance the audit standards, although they need not know when the audit will occur.

The same audit standards can and should be applied to the central files area. In this case, add the following information to the above list of standards:

Number of items filed per month.
Number of items retrieved per month.
Number of items not found per month.

Just as you did with the records center, you can calculate a nonretrieval ratio. The formula, standards, and problem-solving techniques are the same as those already discussed in Chapter 5.

By implementing the practices and controls in this chapter, you'll be able to bring the organization's active records under control. In the next two chapters, we'll see how the same techniques can be applied to the creation of records.

CHAPTER 8

Forms Management: An Integral Part of the Records Program

When we turn our attention to the problem of controlling records from their creation, forms immediately spring to mind as a major component of organizational paperwork. In his book *Business Forms Management,* William Nygren states that 30 percent of all working hours in an average corporation are spent processing forms or reports and that 28 percent of that time (or 8.4 percent of the total working hours) is wasted because of inefficient forms and procedures. Another indication of the growing "forms problem" is that the federal government now measures the time required to complete many forms in weeks or months.

Forms are an especially troubling part of the paperwork explosion because they are self-perpetuating. If you write an unnecessary letter, you've wasted only your own time—once. If you design an unnecessary form, others will repeatedly waste their time completing and processing that form. As a result, forms management was developed to control the organizationwide use of forms.

WHAT IS FORMS MANAGEMENT?

Forms management involves analyzing the users' needs to determine what form (if any) is needed, then designing the best possible form to meet those needs, and finally monitoring all forms used by the organization to insure maximum efficiency in ordering, stocking, and distribution. The overall objectives of the process are to increase organizational efficiency and productivity and to save money in both the production and usage of forms.

Forms management achieves these objectives through the following actions:

Eliminating unnecessary forms, unnecessary copies of forms, and unnecessary items on forms.

Consolidating forms that serve similar purposes.

Preventing unnecessary new forms and unnecessary revisions to existing forms.

Designing forms for maximum effectiveness.

Insuring proper reproduction, stocking, and distribution of forms.

WHERE TO BEGIN

When you start a forms management program at your company, you must choose between two alternative courses of action. The first is simply to take over the forms ordering and reordering functions. You put the new program into effect gradually by consolidating, revising, or eliminating existing forms when they are due for reorder and by designing effective new forms when requested. Because this first alternative will achieve our dual objectives of increased efficiency and reduced expense gradually, it is less desirable than our other option. This second alternative requires a major initial effort, but you reap the benefits much more quickly. You begin by surveying and classifying all corporate forms. Then, starting with the major problem areas revealed by the survey, you consolidate, redesign, and eliminate forms as needed.

CONDUCTING A FORMS SURVEY

Conducting a forms survey is much simpler than conducting a records inventory, because you don't have to visit each department to collect the forms. Instead, you can send out a memo signed by an appropriate top executive, such as the president, introducing the program. Figure 11, an example of such a memo, lists the information you will need about each form.

As you receive each department's forms, check them off on a master list of departments. After the deadline passes, call any

Figure 11. Sample forms survey introduction memo.

To: All department heads
From: (name)

(Company name) is instituting a forms management program to increase our forms' effectiveness, reduce their cost, and eliminate unnecessary paperwork. When the program is fully implemented, our new forms management department, headed by (name), will be responsible for designing and ordering all forms.

The first step in the program is collecting copies of all forms now in use. Please send three copies of each form your department uses to (name, department) by (date—usually two weeks later). On one copy of each form, write the following information:

Your department name,
Whether the form is filled in by machine or by hand.
Where your department obtains the form.
Number of copies of the form your department uses annually
Cost of the form, if known.

Even if another department uses the same form, you should still submit three copies. And remember that a form is any standarized, preprinted means of collecting information, including labels, checks, envelopes, letterhead, questionnaires, and standard contracts.

If you have any questions about the program, please call (name) at (extension).

department heads who have not submitted their forms. Negotiate a deadline extension with them (normally one week) and confirm that deadline in writing. If this deadline is not met, try one last reminder in writing. If you still haven't received the forms one week after the reminder, send a report to your boss and any other appropriate members of upper management listing those departments whose forms you haven't received.

CLASSIFYING THE FORMS

Once you've collected this huge mass of paper, your next job is to organize it. This task involves setting up three different files: numeric, functional, and specifications. These files will become a permanent part of the forms management department.

The Numeric File

As the name implies, the numeric file is arranged by forms number. This historical file will contain all available information about the form: the specifications sheet, order requests, purchase order or print shop requisitions, correspondence relating to the form, several copies of the form, and any other pertinent information. For starters, you'll file here those forms submitted by the various departments that have the form's usage, cost, and so forth written on them.

Developing a forms numbering system. Of course, if no forms numbering system exists, you'll have to develop one before you can establish a numeric file. Almost as many different numbering systems exist as there are forms management departments. The most effective systems, however, tend to be the simplest. You're not trying to capsulize all relevant information about the form in the number, but simply to provide a unique reference number for that form.

Consecutive numbering is the easiest system and generally works well for companies with up to 3,000 forms. Here you simply assign each form a four-digit number, beginning with 0001. For companies with well under 1,000 forms, three-digit numbers may be used.

Since forms are revised frequently and users need an easy way to make sure they have the latest revision, add *A* for the first printed version (1099-A, for example). When the form is revised for the first time, you go to 1099-B, then *C*, and so on. Instead of an alpha code, you can use the revision date, as in 1099-5/82. However, using the revision date makes the number longer. Also, users may feel a perfectly good form is "out of date" because its number includes "6/75."

Another forms numbering system is particularly effective for organizations that are diversified or that have several thousand forms. In these cases, the form can be prefaced with an alpha code. This code can indicate whether the form is for overall corporate use or for use within a particular division. For example, SG1044-A would be a form used in the sporting goods division; CH1044-A, one used in the chemicals division; and CP1044-A, a form for overall corporate use. In this case, the numeric file is set up by alpha code first, and then all forms within that particular code are numbered consecutively. Note, too, that more than one form can have the same number as long as the initial alpha codes are different.

The same system can be used to indicate the particular *function* or subject the form pertains to, such as PER for personnel, MKT for marketing, and so on. However, linking the code to a specific *department* can create problems. If the organization is restructured, the forms numbers may no longer match the departments. Also, departments may feel possessive about *their* forms. They then discourage other departments from using their forms by wanting the forms to be designed exclusively for their needs.

To keep track of the forms numbers as they're assigned, set up a numbering log similar to the one in Figure 12. Or you can store the same information in a computer. Numbers are assigned consecutively. When a form is retired from the ranks, don't reissue the number for several years (at least seven is desirable). Otherwise, confusion can arise as to which form 0710 is being referred to or required.

The Functional File

Your second forms file is the functional file. This file groups forms together by what they do, or their function. When you begin your forms program, this file is a great aid in consolidating or eliminating forms that serve similar purposes. It also helps prevent the creation of unnecessary new forms.

Functional filing systems can be set up on two or three levels. For over 2,000 forms, you'll probably prefer a three-level system. For smaller quantities, a two-level system should suffice.

With either system, the first two levels are the same. The first level is the form's subject, such as accounts payable, customers, employees, invoices, leases, taxes, and vehicles. The second level is the modifier. It amplifies or explains what is done to the subject. Examples are application for, change of, cost of, payment of, and repair of. The third level or function is an action verb, such as to authorize, to cancel, to notify, to report, and to request.

Here's a sample group of functional files:

11-08-22   Equipment, Office—Inventory of—To Record
11-08-31   Equipment, Office—Inventory of—To Verify

FORMS NUMBERS LOG

Form No.	Form Title	Replaces Form No.	Dept./Requester	Date Requested	Date Removed from Use*
1798	Purchase Order Requisition	0681, 0973	Purchasing/T. Smales	6/7/82	

*Completed only when form becomes obsolete.

Figure 12. Forms numbers log.

11-17-03	Equipment, Office—Purchase of—To Authorize
11-17-24	Equipment, Office—Purchase of—To Request
11-20-17	Equipment, Office—Resale of—To Notify
11-28-03	Equipment, Office—Transfer of—To Authorize
11-28-24	Equipment, Office—Transfer of—To Request

As you see, numeric codes are assigned to each item in the functional grouping. Only the digits are recorded on the file folder to simplify typing of labels and filing. Of course, an alpha index for the numbers is necessary. And new items are added to the subject, modifier, and function categories as needed.

Reviewing the files in our example would indicate several possibilities for consolidation. If there is more than one form in any file category, consolidating them would probably be desirable. The forms for recording and verifying inventory might be combined. The request and authorize functions might easily be combined for both purchasing and transferring equipment. And depending on the information needed, the resale and transfer forms might even be combined.

When new forms are requested, the functional file is checked to see if an existing form either meets the need or can be adapted to meet the need. If not, then a new form must be developed.

Unlike the numeric file, the functional file simply contains copies of the forms that exist under each classification. Initially, you'll file one of the copies that was submitted by a user department. Some companies substitute a functional card file listing the form titles and numbers in each category for the actual copies. If space is a problem, you may want to use a card file. Otherwise, having forms in functional file folders saves time going to the numeric file to pull samples. In any case, the numeric file for each form should contain a cross-reference to the appropriate functional file.

The Specifications File

Our third file—the specifications file—is also a money saver. This file contains samples of all existing forms classified by their physical characteristics or construction. Typical categories would be envelopes, continuous forms, snap-out forms, self-adhesive labels, letterhead, chemical carbonless paper, and 8½″ × 11″ padded forms.

A form could conceivably fit in more than one category, as would self-adhesive mailing labels in a continuous roll.

By helping you group appropriate orders, the specifications file enables you to order more economically. For example, assume the president's letterhead is due for reordering. You would then pull the "spec" file for letterhead and determine what other letterheads are printed on the same stock. You'd then check inventory levels on these letterheads. Assume you discovered the air freight division's letterhead should reach reorder level in another two months, but the international division has an eleven-month supply in stock. You would then get air freight's approval to reorder, thus creating a larger order and, as a result, a lower cost for each letterhead than with separate orders. Also, you and the purchasing department now have one order to process instead of two.

You would, however, hold off on the international order because of the extensive supply on hand. Normally you don't want over one year's supply of a form on hand, because if the form must be changed, you would have to destroy too many extra copies. Also, storage costs for the forms would reduce or eliminate the savings from an exceptionally large order.

If you have an automated inventory control system that tells you the supply on hand of any form and notifies you when a form reaches its reorder point, you'll want to build the specifications file into that system. Then, at reorder time, you can "call up" on your terminal the inventory quantities of other forms with the same physical construction and make your decision accordingly.

FORMS ANALYSIS AND DESIGN

Conducting a survey and setting up the appropriate files is the starting point. Now you are ready to begin the ongoing aspects of the program—analysis, design, and control. Analysis identifies the user's needs that must be met by the form, while design uses the information collected from analysis to develop the best possible form. Control is the monitoring of all forms used by the organization to insure their efficient reproduction, stocking, use, and reordering.

Normally one individual—a forms analyst—performs both the analysis and design functions for a particular group of forms.

When these functions are split, information is usually lost in the transfer from analyst to designer. Also, the user often has to work with two people on the same form instead of one.

When either a user requests a new form or the forms management department decides to consolidate or revise certain forms (often as indicated by the functional file), the analyst must first interview the form's requester and/or users.

The Interview

The analyst's interview should provide answers to the following questions regarding the form's content, usage, and physical features.

Content

1. *What information does the user NEED to collect on the form?* Note the emphasis on "need." If an item seems inappropriate or unnecessary, question it. The user should be able to justify every item he or she wants on the form. It's also a good idea to have the user indicate what information is most important.

2. *Can any of the questions on the form have multiple-choice answers?* Listing the various answers saves time in completing the form by reducing the amount of writing. Multiple choices also speed compiling data, as less handwriting has to be deciphered and responses are channeled into a limited number of categories. Of course, you'll use "Other:_____" for situations where other alternatives to the main choices exist.

Usage

1. *How many copies of the form will be used in a year?* You don't want to spend a great deal of time designing a low-usage form (under 300 copies a year)—it simply isn't cost-effective. In these cases, you may even want the user to prepare a rough draft of the form, which you "polish" and incorporate into the system. When only one department uses such a form, you may also want to make that department responsible for storing the form and notifying you when the reorder point is reached.

2. *Who will be completing the form?* What's their educational background and level of familiarity with the material on the form? If, for example, customers will complete the form at home, you need

to provide very complete, simple instructions. The form must truly "stand alone" in these circumstances. On the other hand, with a technical form to be filled out by radiologists at a hospital, users will probably be familiar with the specialized terminology, how to obtain equipment readings, and so forth.

3. *Where will the form be completed—at a desk, in a noisy plant, on a truck?* The conditions under which the form must be completed will affect its physical design. For example, a shop foreman may need a "book" of maintenance forms that can be stuck in a hip pocket, while an insurance clerk at a desk can work well with an 8½" × 11" form.

4. *Who NEEDS copies of the form?* Again, "needs" is the critical word, because you want to keep the number of copies to a minimum. You'll also need to know if the copies will be separated and distributed all at once or piecemeal. Also, you'll need to know whether the copies will be mailed or distributed within the company. All of these factors will affect the form's physical construction.

5. *Does the form relate to other forms, either as a source of information for them or as a result of them?* If it does, get samples of the other forms and explore the possibility of consolidation. Even if you can't consolidate, familiarity with the other forms will help you design this one so data can be transferred easily.

6. *Likewise, is the form a source document for computer input?* If so, it must be developed so that data can be entered correctly and transferred easily. You'll need to know how many spaces are available for each data item, the order in which items will be entered into the computer system, what data will not be entered into the computer, and any special requirements the system has.

Physical Features

1. *Will the form be microfilmed?* If so, you'll want the copy being filmed to be white, as colored paper does not always film well. Likewise, depending on the type of camera, the weight and size of the form can be critical factors. These considerations are discussed in more detail in Chapter 10.

2. *Does the form have any special size requirements?* For example, must it fit in a card file or briefcase?

3. *How will the form be filed—in a binder or file folder?* These factors will affect its size and its margins.

4. *How long will the form be kept?* If it's not filmed, the retention period will help to determine the grade of paper used.

Forms Design

Once the analyst has collected all of the above information, he or she is ready to prepare a rough draft of the form. The first step is sorting all of the desired information into logical groups, such as customer name, address, and phone number. Next, these groups should be arranged in a logical order—logical, that is, for the completer and the processor of the form.

Finally, the rough draft is prepared. This draft should be photocopied and copies given to the user for testing. Testing is probably the most important step in the whole process and should be done for every new or extensively revised form. Even if the user tells you the form looks perfect, test it. Only testing in real world situations will indicate if the form really works. Too many firms have learned this lesson the hard way by printing forms and then discovering problems using them that necessitated starting over.

After the form is tested, you'll make any needed changes and retest if necessary. When the form is finally perfected, it's time for the final layout, typesetting, and printing.

The Eleven Commandments of Forms Design

Forms design is not a difficult or complicated art—not, that is, if you follow these rules. They will help you create forms that are efficient, economical, and attractive.

1. *Use the box, or ULC (upper-left caption), design for captions,* as shown in Figure 13. This design enables you to fit more items into less space, speeds completion when the form is typed by reducing the amount of spacing and tabbing, and reduces the chance of misplaced information. This style does require that the captions be typeset, but that's a minor factor when contrasted with the benefits.

Whenever possible, line up the caption boxes as was done in Figure 13 (box design) with the employee number, home telephone, and zip code. Then the typist can use the same tab stop repeatedly.

Employee Name		Employee Number	
Street Address		Home Telephone	
City	State	Zip Code	

Acceptable: Box, or ULC, design

Employee Name _____

Street Address _____

City _____ State _____ Zip Code _____

Employee Number _____ Home Telephone _____

Unacceptable design
(wastes space and slows typing)

Employee Name   Employee Number

Street Address   Home Telephone

City   State   Zip Code

Unacceptable design
(unclear as to where information should be written)

Figure 13. Acceptable versus unacceptable caption design.

Also, be sure that the captions are clear and descriptive. Words like "name," "number," and "date" may mean one thing to you and another to the person completing the form. For example, on an insurance form, "date" might mean either when the form was completed or when the accident occurred. However, you can abbreviate if the abbreviation will be readily understood (for example, "no." for "number").

2. *Write questions in a multiple-choice format* instead of fill-in-the-blank whenever possible. To reduce confusion, put the check box (□) in front of the item, not behind it, and space accordingly.

Acceptable   □ Excellent   □ Good   □ Fair   □ Poor

Unacceptable Excellent □   Good □   Fair □   Poor □

3. *Leave ample space for writing information* and align the lines so the typewriter carriage does not have to be repeatedly adjusted to match the spacing. For vertical lines, three lines to the inch normally works for both handwriting and double-space typing. However, that measurement does not work for some word processors, so you should test the form on the equipment that will be used to complete it, if possible.

For horizontal spacing, allow two inches for the first ten characters and one inch for every seven to eight additional characters. If you don't know how long a name will be, allow at least three inches. And if the data will be entered into a computer, use "tick marks," not boxes, to indicate the number of spaces in the data field. (Boxes make it difficult to transfer data accurately.)

Acceptable |⎸_|_|_|_|_|_|_|_|_|_|_|_|_|_|_|_|⎸

Unacceptable ▭▭▭▭▭▭▭▭▭▭▭▭▭▭▭▭▭▭

And if you want people to write comments on the form, draw lines for them to write on. The lines motivate the users to write more than a large blank space does. They also help control extremely large or small handwriting and make it easier to read.

4. *Always put the form number in the same place.* There are four schools of thought as to the preferred spot: upper left corner, lower left, upper right, lower right. Although the lower left corner is the

most popular, it doesn't really matter which you choose as long as you're consistent.

5. *Allow at least a ³/₈ inch margin all around the form* and a ³/₄ inch margin on the left-hand side if the form is to be three-hole-punched. The margin serves two purposes. First, printing presses do not normally print to the edges, and extending the lines through "bleeding" is expensive. Second, margins increase the form's readability.

6. *Use visual aids, when appropriate, for emphasis.* For example, use bold or double lines to separate various sections of the form and single lines or hairlines to separate individual items. Use a 20 percent screen (for a lightly shaded effect) to break up columns of figures, to indicate what portion of the form a particular person completes, or to show what data is not entered into the computer. You can also use dingbats to focus attention on specific items. (No, a dingbat is not the late, lamented Edith Bunker but a typographical ornament, such as a dot ●, asterisk *, or arrow ➡.)

7. *Use a sans serif typeface for captions, headings, and short instructions.* Use serif type for lengthy instructions or text. Serifs are the angled lines, or "feet," extending from letters. This book is set in a serif typeface, while the captions on the sample forms are set in sans serif types (that is, without serifs). Helvetica and Univers are commonly used sans serif types, and Century is a popular serif type. Serif type is easier to read in text because the serifs break the monotony, but sans serif is "cleaner" and more effective for headings, captions, and other short items.

8. *Write clear, concise instructions.* And if several steps are involved, list and number them. For example:

To report a theft:
1. Complete sections 1, 2, 3, and 5 of this form.
2. Send the white and yellow copies of this form to your insurance agent, along with a copy of the police form.
3. Keep the green copy for your records.

Ideally, the form should be self-explanatory, so users don't have to refer to a procedures manual to find out how to complete it. If the instructions are too long or too complex to fit on the form itself, you might print them on a thin cover sheet, which can be torn off and referred to while the form is completed. If the forms are contained in a "book," another option is printing the instructions on the inside cover. But never print the instructions on the back of the form. Most people overlook them, and in any case, it's very frustrating to keep having to flip the form over to read them.

9. *If a form is multipart, be sure to indicate the proper distribution order* either in the instructions or at the bottom of the form. It's also a good idea to use different colors for each copy and, if possible, to be consistent in your use of color, so that purchasing, for example, always gets the pink copy. If you will be microfilming the form, design it so that a white copy will be filmed. Also, remember that some colors of paper do not photocopy well.

10. *Use standard-size paper whenever possible* to reduce costs and to use the paper most effectively. Standard sizes are those that can be cut evenly from a 17" × 22" sheet. For example, four 8½" × 11" sheets can be cut evenly from a 17" × 22" sheet. Other standard sizes are 17" × 1", 8½" × 7⅓", 8½" × 5½", and 4¼" × 5½".

11. *Consider using chemical carbonless paper for multicopy forms.* This paper is sometimes incorrectly referred to as NCR (no carbon required) paper, but in reality, NCR is the trademark for Appleton Paper's brand of chemical carbonless paper. One big advantage of chemical carbonless paper is that you can usually print the forms in-house, while carbon-interleaved or snap-out forms must usually be done by an outside printer. Forms printed on chemical carbonless paper take less storage space, are cheaper to ship, and are generally preferred by users because they are less "messy." However, carbon sets can produce more copies and may cost less, depending on the quantity ordered. And some users do report allergies to chemical carbonless paper—apparently a reaction to the formaldehyde released from the tiny dye capsules contained in the paper.

FORMS CONTROL

It's not enough to design the best possible forms. You also need to control the entire forms process. The forms manager must work as a team with not only the users of the forms but also the print shop, the purchasing manager, and the supply room to insure that forms are printed quickly, efficiently, and economically and that they are in stock when needed.

The Printing Decision

The decision as to whether to print in-house or go outside should be based on the in-house print shop's ability to do the work in terms of both equipment and time as well as the comparative cost. If you do use outside vendors for some forms, it is normally the purchasing department's responsibility to select the supplier and monitor the purchasing process. You, however, supply all information about the form's specifications, design, and construction and work directly with the vendor in these areas. You are also responsible for giving purchasing feedback about the vendor's performance.

One option you may want to consider is having an outside firm provide a complete forms management program. A number of vendors provide such programs. These programs are tailored to your company's individual needs, but typically they include:

Designing all forms.
Warehousing the forms.
Providing a complete inventory control service.
Delivering forms to the client as needed.

Depending on your in-house capabilities and your forms volume, you may find such a program to be cost-effective. The major advantage is that it provides you with a complete, professional forms management program that requires much less effort on your part than staffing an in-house function. The major drawback is that you become totally dependent on an outside supplier. If problems develop, it will be difficult and time-consuming to extricate yourself. So if you are considering such a program, test the vendor with a small portion of the company's forms before becoming totally committed.

Determining Order Quantities

Two of your most important decisions in forms ordering are (1) how much to order and (2) when to reorder. Let's consider how much to order first.

As we've already mentioned, you should not order more than one year's supply of any form at a time because the form may need to be revised. For forms with a usage of under 5,000 copies a year, simply order one year's supply. But for forms with a usage of 5,000 or more copies, you should calculate the economic order quantity (EOQ). The EOQ is simply a mathematical formula for determining the most economical amount of any item to order. The formula is:

$$EOQ = \sqrt{\frac{2 \times \text{annual usage of form} \times \text{cost of processing a purchase order}}{\text{cost per form} \times \text{carrying charges}}}$$

The annual usage of the form and the cost per form are self-explanatory. If you wish, you can use cost per 1,000 forms and state the usage in thousands. You will need to obtain from the purchasing department (or the accounting department) the standard cost of processing a purchase order. This will probably be between $30 and $50. The carrying charges figure is the holding cost (warehouse space, overhead, insurance, and so forth) for keeping the item in storage. Your accounting department or supply department should be able to give you this percentage figure. Typically, carrying charges are 20 percent to 30 percent of the inventory value.

Once you've obtained all this information, you're ready to calculate the EOQ—the most economical number of forms to order. If, however, the EOQ is greater than one year's usage, then you'll order one year's usage instead.

Here's an example:

    10 = annual usage in thousands
  $40 = cost of purchase order
  $30 = cost per thousand forms
  20% = carrying charges

$$EOQ = \sqrt{\frac{2 \times 10 \times 40}{30 \times .20}}$$

$$EOQ = \sqrt{133.33}$$

$$EOQ = 11.55$$

Our most economical order would be approximately 11,500 forms. Since this is over one year's usage, we'd order 10,000 forms instead. Now let's assume our annual usage is 50,000 forms and all other figures remain the same.

$$EOQ = \sqrt{\frac{2 \times 50 \times 40}{30 \times .20}}$$

$$EOQ = \sqrt{666.67}$$

$$EOQ = 25.82$$

Our most economical order would be approximately 26,000 forms, or slightly over a half year's usage.

One caution about EOQ—it doesn't allow for seasonal fluctuations in usage. So in the last example, if you typically used 30,000 of the 50,000 forms from October to December, a 26,000-form order would not be satisfactory for that period. In cases such as this, you need to use historical usage patterns as well as the EOQ to insure that you do not run out of a critical form.

Setting Reorder Points

Now that we've determined how many forms to order, we need to determine an appropriate reorder point. Then when the supply room notifies you that that point is reached, you have ample time to get a new shipment in without the form's being out of stock. The factors you'll need to consider in setting a reorder point are:

The time needed for users to approve a reprint or request changes.

The time needed to implement any changes and place the order.

The time needed to print the form on a normal, not rush, basis. (You want to avoid overtime charges if at all possible.)

Amount of safety stock. (Normally your goal is to have one month's supply of the old forms on hand when the new ones are delivered.)

Any seasonal variations in usage.

In most cases, you'll probably find setting the reorder point at a three months' supply will work well. But for heavily used or very important forms, it's a good idea to calculate the reorder point on a case-by-case basis using the above criteria.

Eliminating Obsolete Forms

You'll also need to include a plan for eliminating obsolete forms in your forms control program. Ideally, the users should notify you when a form becomes obsolete. However, if you wait for that to happen, you'll soon have a supply room full of obsolete forms.

Consequently, you'll need to take the initiative. A good policy is to check with the users on all forms that have not been ordered for two years. If you have an automated system, you simply request a list of such forms.

If your program isn't automated, there's a simple and effective manual approach using colored metal or plastic tabs. A different color is used for each year. The first time a form is ordered in a particular year, you attach a colored tab for that year to the numerical folder, such as blue for 1983. Then the next year, you'll attach a different-colored tab the first time any form is ordered, such as red for 1984. At the beginning of the following year (1985, in our example), you simply pull the folders with neither red nor blue tabs and check with their users to see if the form is still needed. Using this process on a regular basis will insure that obsolete forms are removed from stock.

"Bootleg" Forms

Probably the most frequent forms control problem is "bootleg" forms—forms that users design and print on their own without consulting the forms management group. In addition to being expensive and often poorly designed, bootleg forms may duplicate other forms already in existence.

Sometimes bootleg forms come about because the forms management group is not service-oriented, and requesting a new form becomes a bureaucratic nightmare. Or users may think "I only need a few copies, so why bother with forms management." But whatever the reason, the problem is a recurrent one, and a multistep approach is needed to eradicate it.

First, forms management must view itself as a service group. Requesting a new form should be a simple, pleasant, speedy process. Second, the print shop and purchasing must accept only those forms orders that have been approved by forms management.

While these steps will eliminate many bootleg forms, we still have the problem of users' photocopying the forms they design. As long as people have unrestricted access to copiers, you probably won't totally eliminate the problem. However, you can reduce it through the use of departmental forms coordinators—individuals, similar to records coordinators, who serve as a liaison between department members and the forms group. In fact, the same person often serves as both forms and records coordinator.

In addition to notifying forms management of obsolete forms and changes needed in existing forms, the coordinator is on the lookout for bootleg forms. The coordinator's job is not to police or criticize "bootleggers," but simply to set up a meeting between them and the forms analyst. Then the bootleg form can either be incorporated into the system or replaced by an existing form.

CHAPTER 9

Reports Management: Controlling the Latest Paperwork Explosion

While forms are perhaps the most obvious cause of excess paperwork, another formidable contender has entered the arena—namely, the report. With the advent of data processing, we have acquired the capability to classify, arrange, and present large masses of information in virtually an infinite number of combinations.

And we have done just that until the average manager is inundated with reports—some of great importance, others "not worth the paper they're written on." The report has also become a corporate status symbol for some insecure managers. They feel they need to be on every distribution list to demonstrate their importance in the corporate hierarchy.

As a result, the report has moved from being a useful information tool to becoming a major problem area. Reports management reverses that trend by controlling the production of reports and insuring that they provide the maximum benefit to the organization.

WHAT KINDS OF REPORTS?

Since we've identified computer-generated reports as the major cause of the reports explosion, it might seem logical to assume that reports management should deal exclusively with these reports. However, the scope of the program should be broadened to also include all manually generated reports that are sent between departments on a repeated basis. Why? Because although they are fewer in number, manually generated reports can also waste a great deal of time and money. And the time wasted is often high-dollar executive time.

Here's a classic example. At one company, the president decided to send the board of directors monthly reports about the company's progress. Sounds like a good idea, doesn't it? Well, in a little over a year, the report grew from 15 pages to over 100. It became a competition between the eight vice-presidents who submitted data to see who could produce the longest section and include the most graphs. The legal department would take two pages just to explain that there had been no change in the cases in litigation. Producing the report tied up the corporate communications staff for over a week each month and reduced the print shop to chaos, as there were always last minute changes.

And what did the recipients think? When one board member was asked for his opinion, he politely said, "It's a nice report, but I've got my own business to run. I don't have time to read all that." A much better alternative would have been a concise two- to three-page summary of key changes since the past month. But as so often happens, the recipients' needs were forgotten by the producers of the report.

Because many situations similar to this exist, regular interdepartmental manual reports should be included in your program. But don't worry about one-time or intradepartmental reports, such as a comparative analysis of some new word processing equipment or an employee's monthly progress report to his or her boss. These reports should be left up to the discretion of the individual manager. Your concern is with those reports that consume significant amounts of time and money.

OBJECTIVES

Just as with forms management, the two primary goals of reports management are to improve efficiency and save money. These goals are achieved through the following processes:

Eliminating unnecessary reports. All too many reports are still produced long after the need for them has ended. The initial reports management effort must "clean house" to eliminate all such reports. Thereafter, all reports must be regularly reevaluated and their continued existence justified.

Consolidating reports whenever possible. Are several departments requesting similar, but not identical, reports? If so, you should investigate consolidating them. Demonstrating to the departments the cost savings of the consolidation will help motivate them to work with you.

Redesigning the contents of reports to increase their effectiveness. Such redesign can include eliminating unnecessary data and adding useful information. It can also mean rearranging items on the report so they'll be easier for the user to work with.

One caution, though, with computer-generated reports: You need to compare the cost of making the change with the benefits it provides. Sometimes a change that seems simple to you may be costly to implement because of the way the initial programming was done or because that programming was never properly documented. So be realistic here. Of course, with manual reports, redesign is comparatively easy and should be done whenever necessary.

Limiting distribution of reports when appropriate. Everyone who receives a report should need that report as part of his or her job. If the need isn't there, the report shouldn't be either. Actually, many people appreciate this aspect of reports management. They often realize that they don't need the report but won't say so for fear it would appear that they're not doing their jobs as thoroughly as they might be.

Some managers have no real need for the report but will say, "I need to check my data against it occasionally." Others may feel that they lose status if they don't have access to the report. For both groups, there's a simple solution. Keep copies of the reports on file at the company library or information center. Then if these managers do want to see the report occasionally, they can. Such a center will also allow managers to reduce their in-office active storage of copies of these reports.

Limiting the number of copies produced. There's a tendency on the part of many managers to order excessive numbers of copies of reports. For example, the manager might decide, "We'll need seven copies—one each for Joe, Sally, Ted, Alice, and Bob, and a couple for the files." Such thinking greatly increases report production costs.

In cases where users do not have to see the report immediately after it is generated or will not be working extensively from the report, copies can be routed. In our example, Joe and Sally might share one copy, which is eventually filed; while Ted, Alice, and Bob might share another. We're now down to two copies. And if someone does occasionally need to keep a page to work with it further, it can always be photocopied.

Reducing the frequency of reports when appropriate. Some reports are produced more often than necessary. At one company, sales reports were produced daily, weekly, and monthly. By the time the daily reports were received, they were out of date. The users concentrated on the weekly and monthly reports. Hence, eliminating the daily report was a logical step.

Also, some users didn't need the weekly report. Another easy change was sending them the monthly copy only. Instances like these are not uncommon. There's a tendency to base a report's frequency on how often we are capable of preparing it instead of how often we need to prepare it.

Exploring microfilm and -fiche applications. With COM (computer output microfilm), computer-generated reports can be printed on film or fiche instead of paper. In Chapter 10, we'll discuss the advantages and applications of COM.

Examining other ways to use office automation to increase the effectiveness of reports and reduce their cost. For example, if users have an electronic work station or terminal, the report can be sent by "electronic mail," even if the users are at another location. The users can then scan the report on their terminal screens and print only the portions they need.

Many manual reports can be prepared on a word processor with new or revised data inserted when approriate rather than having a secretary retype the entire report each time it is reissued. Intelligent copier/printers (also known as electronic printers) can quickly produce copies that appear "typeset" from either an on-line word processor or computer or from off-line magnetic media. Some intelligent copier/printers can also prepare the report on microfiche instead of paper. Because modern office technology is improving constantly, you should monitor this area for new developments.

SELLING THE REPORTS MANAGEMENT CONCEPT

Selling reports management to the company's upper management group is relatively easy because of the program's cost effectiveness. Most organizations are not aware of what they're spending on reports. Once they become aware of that cost and once they realize reports management can usually save a minimum of 10 percent of that figure and probably much more, they become quite receptive to the idea.

Also, the decision makers—senior management—are also the group that usually gets the heaviest barrage of reports. These individuals know they have problems coping with the influx of reports, and they tend to welcome help.

Just as with records management in general, you can sell the reports management program more easily if you find and document one or two "horror stories." Look for some high-cost reports that are overdistributed and poorly designed. Then show how these reports could be improved and the resulting cost savings. Explain that you want to apply that same concept on a larger scale, concentrating on those reports that cost the most to produce.

Middle management will be a tougher nut to crack. There will be fear that you're "taking over" their reports and trying to limit the information they receive. You must convince them that reports management is identical in concept to forms management and that your goal is to make information more accessible and more economical.

Also, if departments are "charged back" for the reports they receive, they'll be more receptive to your idea. It will also help if your department has already gained credibility and trust through the successful implementation of other aspects of records management.

WHERE TO BEGIN

A reports management program begins in much the same way as forms management or records retention does—with an inventory.

Your task in collecting this data will be simplified somewhat because many of the reports will be generated by one department—data processing.

Consequently, it's a good idea to have someone from data processing assigned to work with you on implementing the reports management program. This individual should collect a sample of each report produced by data processing and should provide the following information for each report:

Report number.
Title.
Department requesting the report.
Frequency of distribution.
Distribution list.
Preparation and printing costs.
Distribution cost (mailing or hand delivery).

Either you or the representative from data processing will then need to contact the department requesting the report to determine its purpose or reason for existence. A form similar to Figure 14 can be used to collect this data.

The same types of information will need to be collected for manually prepared reports. In this case, the department originating the report will complete the form and submit it to you along with a sample copy of the report. The one area on the form that will differ between computer-generated and manual reports is cost. With manual reports, instead of data processing costs, you will record the hours of managerial, secretarial, and clerical time spent preparing the report, as well as other costs, such as postage and printing or photocopying.

You'll then need to convert the managerial, secretarial, and clerical hours to dollars by using standard hourly rates for each category. You can obtain these rates from personnel, and you should make sure that they include an allowance for fringe benefits.

RANKING THE REPORTS

After you've collected the survey data, the next step is to rank the reports in order of decreasing cost. Ranking is important, because you'll want to concentrate your primary efforts on the most costly

REPORTS INVENTORY			
Report Title			
Dept. Requesting or Originating Report			

Purpose of report: _____

Frequency	**Distribution (indicate if more than one copy sent)**		
☐ daily ☐ semiannually	Name	Department	No. of Copies
☐ weekly ☐ annually			
☐ monthly ☐ other _____			
Cost (use average figures)			
EDP costs (if any) _____			
Printing/photocopying _____			
Mailing _____			
Graphics _____			
Word processing _____			
Other _____ _____			
_____ _____			
Total _____			
Time (do *not* include EDP time computed above)			
Hrs. managerial _____			
Hrs. secretarial _____			
Hrs. clerical _____			
Hrs. other _____			
Completed by	Dept.		Date

Figure 14. Reports inventory.

reports. It's not practical to spend 10 to 20 hours redesigning a report that costs $300 a year to prepare, print, and publish. If the report costs $30,000 a year, however, the time spent redesigning it is easy to justify.

To further classify your reports, you can use a variation of Pareto's law. That is, you can assume 20 percent of your reports will account for approximately 80 percent of your total reports expenditures. Consequently, devote your primary efforts toward improving these reports, which can be termed your "A"-reports.

You'll want to spend less time on the remaining reports, again working in order of descending cost. You may even set a cutoff point, such as $500 a year. For reports costing less than this amount to produce, the only decision you'll make is whether or not the report continues to exist.

INTERVIEWING THE RECIPIENTS

The next step is interviewing the recipients of the A-reports, either in person or by phone. The cost of producing the A-reports justifies the time and money spent on the interviews. People tend to be more candid in an interview than when completing a questionnaire, and you, in turn, have an opportunity to sell people on the benefits of the reports management program. In-person interviews are preferable to those conducted over the phone, as you can identify problems more easily. However, if the report's recipients are at another site, you may have to use the phone.

Use Figure 15 or a similar form to record the interview data. You'll prepare one form for each recipient of each report. If one person receives several A-reports, cover all of the reports in one interviewing session, using a separate form for each.

When conducting the interview, begin by asking how the report is used, not whether it's needed, as some people may be reluctant to admit they don't need the report. If the recipient indicates that he or she just "reviews" the report and doesn't take action based on it, then suggest sharing a routed copy or having access to a "library" copy. For those recipients who indicate no need at all for the report, explain that you'll have them removed from the distribution list and end the interview.

The other questions on the form are self-explanatory. However,

REPORT RECIPIENT QUESTIONNAIRE
To be completed by report recipient or interviewer

Report Title		Report No.

Recipient	Department	Phone

1. Do *you* still need the report?   ☐ Yes   ☐ No

   a. If "yes," explain briefly how you use the report.

   _____

   _____

   b. If "no," don't complete remainder of form.

2. Do *you* need to receive the report as frequently as you do now?

   ☐ Yes   ☐ No

   If "no," how frequently do you need to see the report?

   ☐ daily   ☐ monthly   ☐ annually

   ☐ weekly   ☐ semiannually   ☐ other _____

3. How can this report be improved? _____

   _____

   _____

   _____

   _____

   _____

   _____

Prepared by	Date

Figure 15. Report recipient questionnaire.

when you ask about improvements to the report, do make it clear that you're not promising that the changes will be made, only that they'll be considered.

Although interviews are preferable for recipients of A-reports, if your resources are extremely limited, you can send the form out as a questionnaire. For recipients of B-reports (the others), you'll probably use the questionnaire approach, as it's difficult to cost-justify interviews in these circumstances.

When you send questionnaires out, fill in each report's title and number. Attach a cover letter, preferably signed by the president or other senior executive, explaining the objectives of the reports management program. The letter should ask the recipients to complete the questionnaire and return it in 30 days. To insure that recipients do return the form, the letter should state that if their replies are not received, they will be automatically removed from the distribution list for that report. Then follow through accordingly.

IMPLEMENTING THE PROGRAM

After you're received all of the responses or conducted the interviews, you can begin taking appropriate action. If no one needs the report, it should be eliminated. Names should be dropped from the distribution list whenever possible and frequency of distribution reduced. These are all easy actions—quick fixes.

Changes in content and design are somewhat more difficult to accomplish. If the report is computer-generated, meet first with your data processing liaison to determine the cost/practicality of the changes. If they seem reasonable, then have a meeting with all users of the report to get their feedback and approval. With manually generated reports, meet with the preparer(s) to see what would be involved in making the changes. Again, if they seem feasible, then meet with all recipients for their feedback and approval.

When this process is completed for all A-reports, your program will be well under way. Then move on the B-reports. Here be sure the time spent improving the report is in proportion to the cost and the benefits.

AN ONGOING PROGRAM

Your next step is to prepare a report for management documenting the changes that were made and the annual cost savings. This report should also include a proposal for an ongoing reports management program. A key part of this ongoing program is the policy that all computer-generated and interdepartmental manual reports that are prepared repeatedly must be approved by the reports management staff. Likewise, all proposed changes in a report's distribution, frequency, or content must be cleared through reports management.

To stop "bootleg" reports, the data processing staff must have instructions to check with the reports management group before preparing any new reports. Your forms or records coordinators can also be responsible for reporting any unauthorized reports in their areas. As a further control device, manual reports, as well as computer-generated ones, should be assigned official report numbers. Then any report without a number is immediately suspect.

The numbering system for manual reports should be a simple one. You can either tie it in with the existing system for computer reports or model it on the numbering systems used for forms in Chapter 8. Just preface each report number with an *R* or other code to indicate that the number refers to a report.

It's also a good idea to classify each report functionally, using a system similar to the functional form file discussed in Chapter 8. Then when there is a request for a new report, you check the functional file to see if an existing report either meets the need or can be adapted to meet it.

REEVALUATING THE REPORTS

The steps just outlined are a good start for an ongoing program, but they aren't enough. Just as you can't depend on the users of a form to notify you when they no longer need it, neither can you depend on the users of a report to do the same.

Thus, every two years, you need to reevaluate any report that has not been changed or reviewed in that period. This review is performed by sending each recipient a questionnaire similar to Figure 15. Again, to insure compliance, you'll explain that they'll be removed from the distribution list if they don't reply in 30 days. This regular review will insure that reports do not live on long after the need for them is gone.

One other technique you can use for eliminating unnecessary reports is the "see if anyone notices it's gone" strategy. You simply don't send out the report and see who calls to complain. Those who don't call are removed from the distribution list. While this technique has worked successfully for many companies, you should have appropriate management support before using it. And don't try it with any reports that are clearly vital to the organization's operations and well-being.

WORKING WITH THE EDP STAFF

For a reports management program to be successful, the records management group must work closely with data processing. In fact, in some companies, reports management is a data processing responsibility. However, this often means that manually prepared reports are excluded from the program. Also, records management skills are required to run the program successfully. Thus, unless records management and data processing are totally merged, these skills may be lacking.

Although records management should have control of the program, data processing must support it if it is to be a success. And you will need a basic understanding of data processing if you are to communicate effectively with this area and evaluate accurately the information you receive from it.

Several things will help to improve your relations with data processing. First, the data processing person assigned to work with you should:

Be committed to the program's success.

Have a broad-based knowledge of both the data processing system and the company as a whole.

Be able to devote most of his or her time to the program until the survey is completed.

Second, if you aren't familiar with data processing, you need to broaden your knowledge in that area. Take a seminar or college course in the fundamentals or read up on the subject. (See the Bibliography for recommendations.) This knowledge is essential, as records management and data processing continue to move closer together.

Third, be realistic. You'll have to consider not only the cost of making a change but also the practicality. If the data processing department is overextended and understaffed, as is so often the case, then it may take time and continual follow-up to get relatively simple changes made. Top management support is also needed here.

All in all, though, reports management is one of the easiest aspects of records management to promote, because it is cost-effective and because top management sees its benefits directly as the number of reports it has to cope with diminishes.

CHAPTER 10

Micrographics and Records Management

Microfilm is one of the most valuable aids a records manager can have for storing and retrieving data. But before we discuss the subject in depth, let's define a few terms. "Microfilm" is a fine-grain, high-resolution film that can record images greatly reduced in size. "Micrographics" refers to the science or art of recording images on microfilm. And "microform" is the generic name for any of the various forms in which microfilm occurs.

ADVANTAGES OF MICROFILM

When we think of the advantages of microfilm, space saving immediately springs to mind. Microfilmed records can save up to 98 percent of the space occupied when the records are kept on paper. This space saving is also reflected in a need for less filing equipment.

But a bigger advantage is often increased productivity. Data on film is physically more accessible and, hence, can be referenced more quickly than data on paper. For example, a seated customer service representative can retrieve and reference a file without leaving his or her desk or even putting down the phone. Also, because records can be duplicated easily and inexpensively, data can be made available to those who need it. And if a paper copy is needed—to send to a customer, for example—it can be reproduced quickly and easily.

Another advantage is improved security. As discussed in Chapter

6, duplicate filmed copies can be stored off-site for a minimal cost. Also, misfiling the documents or disrupting their order is less likely because they are filmed in a fixed, unalterable sequence. And if properly filmed, microfilm is generally admissible as evidence in a court of law. However, there are some exceptions to film's legality, which we'll discuss later in this chapter.

Other advantages are that film is more durable than paper and can be mailed much more cheaply. Also, it can be used instead of paper as a medium for computer printouts.

LIMITATIONS OF MICROFILM

Although microfilm has many advantages, there are also some definite limitations that must be considered when you're deciding whether data should be stored on paper, on microfilm, or on-line in a computer. The most obvious limitation is the need for a reader to access the data kept on film. Readers are cheaper than computer terminals, but they are still a mechanical barrier that a paper system does not have.

There are also limitations as to what can be filmed. Depending on the type of camera, certain documents are too large to be filmed. If a document is in poor condition, it will not film well. Colored paper can present problems that must be compensated for, as does very thin paper, such as onionskin.

Updating can also present problems unless you are using an updatable microfiche system. And of course, you can't write notes on a microfilm copy as you can on paper. Cost can also be a limitation. In most cases, you shouldn't convert to microfilm unless you can cost-justify it. However, cost-justification has become easier. Micrographics equipment has improved in quality and decreased in price, while the costs of maintaining paper systems have risen.

MICROFORMS

Before we can discuss developing a microfilm system, you need to become familiar with the various forms microfilm can take, the equipment options, and the ways the film can be created. Let's begin by examining the various microforms and their applications.

Serialized Microforms

Serialized microforms are so named because documents are accessed sequentially; that is, you must go through the roll of film until you reach the image you want. These microforms work well when you are filming documents in sequential order, such as a series of numbered invoices, and do not plan to make additions in the middle of the series.

Serialized microforms are desirable for labor-intensive input situations. That is, they work well when large amounts of material must be filmed rapidly and the retrieval frequency is relatively low. When we discuss cameras, you'll understand why serialized filming can be performed rapidly. And of course, retrieval is slowed because the roll of film must be advanced to the desired image.

The three types of serialized, or roll-film, microforms are illustrated in Figure 16. They are open-reel, cartridge, and cassette film.

Open-reel film. Open-reel film was one of the first microforms. Just as the name implies, it is an open spool of microfilm. Open-reel film is the least expensive microform and is most commonly used in 16-mm and 35-mm widths. Reel film that is 105 mm wide is normally cut into microfiche. The 16-mm film is normally used for correspondence, checks, and letter- or legal-size documents. The 35-mm film is used for graphics and for large documents, such as X-rays, newspapers, and maps.

Unless self-threading readers are used, open-reel film is difficult to thread into the reader. Also, open-reel readers are more expensive than microfiche readers. Consequently, open-reel film is generally best suited for low-reference situations.

Cartridges. Cartridges, or magazines, represent a refinement of the open-reel concept. Here the roll of film is encased in plastic to protect it. Cartridges are easy to work with and can be threaded into the reader without difficulty. However, you need a reader that is compatible with the particular brand of cartridge you are using. In other words, once you choose a particular cartridge system, you are pretty well "locked into" that vendor. As might be expected, cartridges are more expensive than open-reel film, and once again, the readers are more expensive than microfiche readers.

Cassettes. Unlike cartridges, cassettes have two reels encased in plastic. Hence, the film is well protected and never leaves the

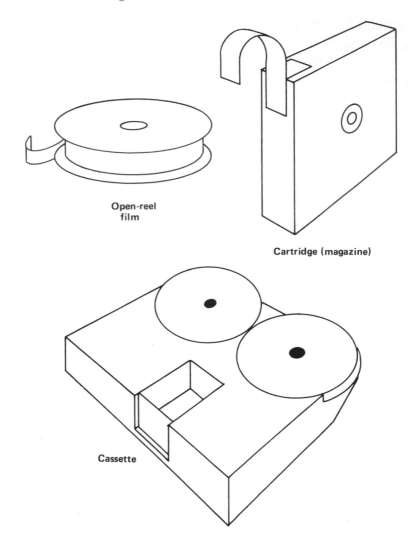

Open-reel film

Cartridge (magazine)

Cassette

Figure 16.Serialized microforms.

cassette. Cassettes do not need to be rewound before being re-moved from the reader. Consequently, a particular image can be left exposed when the cassette is removed. Like cartridges, cassettes require readers that are compatible with that particular brand. And again, the readers are considerably more expensive than microfiche readers. Also, because of the two reels, cassettes are relatively bulky and take up significantly more storage space than cartridges.

Unitized Microforms

Unlike their serialized counterparts, unitized microforms permit direct access to data without advancing through the roll of film. Unitized microforms are easy for users to work with, can be indexed in a variety of ways, and require less expensive readers than the various types of roll film. Also, many readers can be used for more than one type of unitized film.

Consequently, unitized microforms are well suited for situations where more effort is expended referencing records than filming them. The main unitized categories—aperture cards, card jackets, microjackets, and microfiche—are shown in Figure 17.

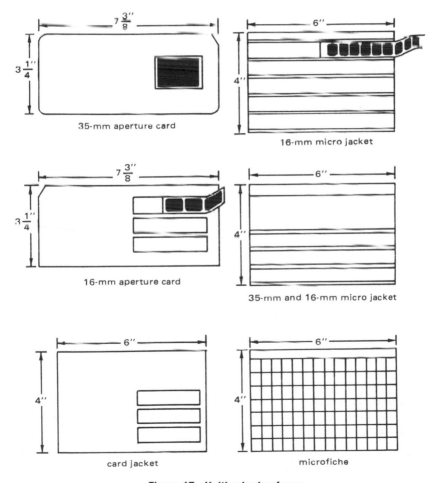

Figure 17. Unitized microforms.

Aperture cards. Aperture cards permit the combination of key-punched data, eyeball-readable information, and microfilm in one format. The cards are most frequently used for storing engineering drawings. The drawing is reproduced on one frame of 35-mm film, which is either affixed to the card or inserted in a plastic "sleeve." Aperture cards that hold strips of 16-mm film are also available.

Card jackets. The card jacket is an index card with sleeves for inserting strips of 16-mm film. This format permits the combination of eyeball-readable data and filmed images. A typical use is a personnel file. Frequently referenced data—such as address, phone number, Social Security number, and job title—are instantly readable, while other documentation, such as appraisals, is filmed. Depending on the format, a card jacket can hold as many as 30 microimages.

Microjackets. The microjacket is a plastic carrier with sleeves for inserting film. The jacket, in effect, allows you to convert roll film to a microfichelike format. It also provides an updatable format, as additional strips of film can be added as needed until the jacket is full. The film is inserted mechanically by a machine known as a jacket loader.

While jackets holding only 16-mm film are most commonly used, jackets that hold both 16-mm and 35-mm film are also available. These jackets can be used to combine engineering drawings and supporting data in one easily duplicatable package.

Microfiche. Our final unitized microform is the most commonly used—microfiche. A microfiche is a sheet of film containing a number of images or frames in a grid pattern. The reduction level determines the number of frames. For example, if documents are filmed at 24X (reduced to $1/24$ of their original size), the equivalent of 98 $8\frac{1}{2}'' \times 11''$ sheets can be held on one fiche. If the reduction level is 42X ($1/42$ of original size), 208 frames can fit on one fiche. And at 48X, the fiche will hold 270 frames. A 24X reduction is common for source-document (hard-copy) microfilming. Computer-output microfiche is commonly done at 42X or 48X, and in some cases it is done at 72X.

One of the disadvantages of microfiche had been the inability to update it or add new documents to a fiche. However, in the 1970s, updatable microfiche became available. With such fiche, additional documents can be filmed on the master copy as desired, thus making the microfiche the equivalent of a growing paper file.

Updatable microfiche has proved successful for personnel records; insurance policyholder files; customer files; and other expanding, frequently referenced files. At this time, there are only three types of updatable microfiche on the market. Of these, one is erasable; that is, existing documents can be completely removed from the fiche. On the other two types, documents can have "void" printed across their face, or they can be totally blacked out. But it will always be apparent that a document was there.

If you select a completely erasable system, you should consider the legal ramifications. A very few regulatory agencies will not accept erasable fiche. This isn't a logical decision, as they will accept paper files. And it's even easier to destroy a document from a paper file without leaving a trace. But logic aside, you want your film to be legally acceptable. Consequently, you'll want to verify that erasable fiche is acceptable at the agencies you work with.

CAMERAS

The microform(s) you decide to use will determine the type of camera you need. And no one camera can produce all the different microforms just described. The cameras do, however, fall into two main categories: rotary and planetary.

Rotary Cameras

Rotary cameras are the more commonly used of the two categories. The name "rotary" refers to the fact that the document and the film move simultaneously during the filming process, creating an effect of "no motion." The documents to be filmed are fed into the camera either manually or automatically. Then both documents and film advance together, and the documents emerge from the camera.

Most rotary cameras use 16-mm film in open-reel, cartridge, or cassette format. And as we've already seen, 16-mm open-reel film can be cut into strips for use in card jackets, microjackets, and 16-mm aperture cards.

Rotary cameras are noted for their speed, with the capability of filming 10,000 to 14,000 8½″ × 11″ documents or 100,000 checks in an eight-hour shift. Some models will film both sides of a document simultaneously—a process known as "duplex" filming. Other models film only one side—"simplex" filming. Most rotary cameras have an automatic exposure control—a very desirable option, as it allows the camera to automatically compensate for paper of different colors.

Obviously, rotary cameras do limit filming to single-sheet documents that can be "fed" through the machine. Brittle or very thin paper also presents problems, as it does not advance smoothly through the camera. Rotary cameras also have limits as to the width of paper they can accept. The models with the widest document feeds can handle paper up to 18 inches wide.

Planetary Cameras

Planetary cameras are so named because both the document and the film remain stationary during the filming process. The material to be filmed is placed on a copy board with exterior lighting mounted on both sides. The filming unit (the actual camera portion of the equipment) is mounted above the copy board and can be raised or lowered to change the reduction level. The resulting image is of a higher quality than that produced by a rotary camera because both the document and paper remain stationary.

Planetary cameras come in a variety of sizes. The larger models can handle documents up to 45 inches wide and are used for filming engineering drawings and other oversize documents. Smaller, tabletop planetary cameras may be used for filming bound books and documents too fragile to pass through a rotary camera, as well as single sheets of paper. Depending on the model, the planetary camera may use either 16-mm or 35 mm-film. Engineering drawings and other similarly sized documents are filmed on 35-mm film.

As might be expected, filming with a planetary camera is generally much slower than with a rotary. Small planetary cameras with automatic document feeds are the exception to the rule. The large planetary models are also considerably more expensive than the average rotary camera.

Step-and-Repeat Cameras

Step-and-repeat cameras are a variation of the planetary camera. These cameras prepare microfiche by exposing a series of separate images on the film according to a previously established format or grid. The camera "steps" the film into position for the next exposure and then "repeats" the filming process. Depending on the model, the step-and-repeat camera uses either 105-mm roll film, which is subsequently cut into microfiche, or sheets of fiche-size film.

Camera Processors

A variety of camera processors are also available. These units film the material and develop the film so that a ready-to-use piece of film emerges. Some models prepare strips of 16-mm film, which can then be loaded into microjackets. Updatable microfiche is prepared in a special camera processor that in appearance and operation is somewhat similar to a large photocopier.

READERS

You don't have to buy or lease a camera to use microfilm. You can instead hire a service bureau to film your material for you. But you must have readers or viewers on-site if you're going to use microfilm.

When selecting a reader, your first consideration is that it will be compatible with the microforms you will be viewing. Microfiche readers can be obtained that will also accept aperture cards, card jackets, and microjackets. With the serialized formats, readers are generally not as versatile. Cartridge and cassette readers will usually accept only one brand of film, although some readers are now available that can be converted to handle more than one serialized format.

Readers should be chosen to fit the individual user's needs and special requirements, not simply purchased *en masse* to save money. Depending on where the reader will be used and the type of microform, the best choice might be a hand-held reader, a portable model, a desk-top unit, or even a large freestanding model. Some hand-held and portable models can operate off batteries or a car's cigarette lighter. And other models will fit in a desk drawer, thus keeping the desk-top work area free for other tasks.

Another consideration is whether the reader will be used for extended periods of time or for quick referencing. If viewing is for extended periods of time, a "blowback" of 100 percent or more is normally desirable. In other words, the image appears as large as or larger than the original document. However, if viewing is for short periods and the type of the original is large enough, a blowback of 75 percent might be adequate.

Also, if viewing is for extended periods, it's important to have a screen angle that is comfortable for the user. Some readers even have tiltable screens. A matte- or dull-finish screen is easier on the eyes, but a shiny finish provides a sharper image. And some users prefer tinted screens for extended viewing.

Other factors you should consider are the sharpness of the screen image, the illumination, and the focus. The screen image should be uniformly sharp and readable over the entire screen area. The screen's illumination should be comfortable for sustained reading without being either too bright or too dim. And the illumination should be fairly even over the entire screen. The reader should be easy to focus, and you shouldn't need to refocus frequently when moving from image to image.

The reader should also be sturdily constructed. In particular, the base should be heavy and large enough to insure that the reader won't be tipped over easily. Maintenance, such as changing bulbs, should be easy to do. And if the unit is a portable, it should be able to withstand drops, bumps, or other "hard knocks."

Keeping all of these factors in mind will help you select readers that are right for the system's users. And one last tip—if you're seriously considering a particular model, ask for a "loaner" for a week or two so the users can work with it and see if it meets their on-the-job requirements.

READER-PRINTERS

In addition to projecting the image on a screen, reader-printers can also make paper copies of a document. The exact nature of the copying process depends on the model, with some using coated paper and others plain paper.

When selecting a reader-printer, you'll want to apply all the criteria discussed under "readers," as they are equally relevant here. You'll also want to evaluate sample prints from several models to see which you prefer and how the quality compares. Another consideration is print size, which, depending on the model, may range from $8\frac{1}{2}'' \times 11''$ to $20'' \times 30''$ or even larger. And finally, you'll want to compare cost per print.

Reader-printers cost much more than readers, which is one reason you should be sure a reader-printer, and not just a reader, is needed in a particular situation. Also, a danger with reader-printers is that users will make unnecessary copies—copies that cost money and may get filed, thus destroying the paper reduction benefits of the film system. To insure that users do not indulge in excessive copies, limit the number of reader-printers and have a trained operator make the copies. This system will cut waste from improperly made copies, as well as insuring that copies are made only when needed. And if hard copies are really needed extensively, then a microfilm system may not be a good idea.

COM

Up to now, we've primarily been discussing source-document microfilming—converting hard copy to film. However, microfilm can also be generated by computers, thus replacing bulky printouts. Computer-output microfilm (COM) is created by a COM recorder. If the system is on-line, the recorder receives data directly from the computer and functions as an output device. If the system is off-line, a magnetic tape is mounted on the recorder's tape drive. In either case, the recorder, in effect, replaces the computer's printer.

Depending on the unit, COM recorders can create 16-mm, 35-mm, or 105-mm film (microfiche). Some units are "universal" and can produce all three sizes. But in any case, the majority of COM is prepared on microfiche. While the most common reduction ratios are 42X and 48X, some units can now produce COM at 72X—the equivalent of 690 pages on one microfiche. And the more tightly the data can be packed on the film, the greater the potential for cost and space savings.

How COM Works

Depending on the model, COM recorders will create the image on film in one of four ways. The CRT (cathode ray tube) technique is the oldest and most commonly used method. A page appears on a CRT screen within the recorder and is exposed to the film. Then the film is advanced, the next page recorded, and so on. With electron beam recording (EBR), an electron beam "writes" the characters on the film. As with the CRT technique, the process is completed on a page-by-page basis. Laser beam recording (LBR) also permits direct "writing" on the film, in this case by a laser beam, and again, on a page-by-page basis. The fourth method, light emitted diode (LED) recording, uses fiber optics to generate a line of characters to which the film is exposed. Then the next line is formed, the film exposed, and so on.

Regardless of the system, the end result is the same—exposed film, which is then processed in an automated film developer. The resulting master copy can then be duplicated as needed for distribution.

Some COM recorders function exclusively as alphanumeric printers. Others are also capable of plotting lines and graphics, with precision models producing graphics of very high resolution and reliability. Another option is the use of forms overlays during the recording process, so that the data appear on the "form" just as they would if they were printed on a hard copy of the form.

Advantages of COM

As you can see, COM recorders have a wide range of capabilities. And the resulting COM documents have several advantages over their hard-copy counterparts. These include:

1. *Economy.* Film is approximately 80 percent cheaper than computer paper. (Remember, we're comparing over 200 pages of printout to one fiche.)
2. *Space savings.* COM reports use 1 percent to 2 percent of the space occupied by their paper counterparts. Of course, if the report is a daily "throwaway," the space savings may not be a significant advantage.
3. *Faster retrieval.* COM can make it practical for users to keep large reports at their fingertips instead of in a bookcase. And the reports can be inexpensively duplicated for everyone who needs them.
4. *Printing speed.* COM recorders print faster than many paper printers.
5. *Less postage.* If the reports are to be mailed, COM is substantially cheaper than paper.

6. *Faster preparation.* COM reports do not need to be decollated, burst, or bound.
7. *No need for separate forms.* As we've already mentioned, forms overlays eliminate the need for separate forms.
8. *Copy quality.* COM copies are of high quality and easy to read.

Limitations of COM

Of course, COM is not the answer to every information need. Data that must be continually updated, such as inventory or reservations systems, is better suited to on-line applications. And naturally, COM has the limitations of microfilm we discussed earlier, such as the need for readers.

You're also more likely to encounter user resistance with COM than with microforms. The reason is simple: COM brings microfilm into the executive suite. While relatively few top executives deal with source-document microfilm, they do deal with computer reports. And when those computer reports are little pieces of plastic that can only be read through a machine instead of large sheets of paper that can be written on and sent to people, the initial reaction is one of frustration.

Usually the best approach is to emphasize the substantial cost savings. Money does talk. Also be aware that a reader-printer may need to be available for executives with frequent hard-copy needs. Now, you may be fortunate and not encounter executive resistance. But don't be surprised if you do. The problem occurs frequently, especially with executives who have negative perceptions of microfilm because they were exposed to an early, poor-quality system.

Another concern is where the COM function belongs in the organization. One school of thought is that it belongs under the jurisdiction of the micrographics department and consequently is part of records management. The other school opts for positioning COM in the data processing or management information services area.

Arguments can be made for both sides. If the system is on-line, it will probably come under the data processing sphere of influence. If it's off-line, it may still fall in that area because of the need to program the tapes so that the format will be suitable for COM. On the other hand, developing and duplicating the film is traditionally a micrographics function. In reality, COM is more likely to be a data processing function because the developing and processing of the film has been greatly simplified with improved technology while the programming is still a key concern. But wherever the responsibility lies, a successful COM program requires smooth interaction between data processing and records management. When that situation does not exist, problems arise.

Another consideration with COM—if you're planning to create it in-house—is its initial cost. COM recorders are quite expensive, and you can easily be looking at a start-up investment of $100,000 or more. For this reason, many companies find it more economical to have a service bureau produce COM from their tapes.

To find a good service bureau, check with other users in your area, particularly fellow ARMA and NMA members. You'll need to perform your own cost calculations to determine if a service bureau is cheaper than an in-house operation. A good general rule is to begin considering in-house COM when your monthly service bureau bill is approximately $5,000. Some companies will convert to in-house COM before it's cost-justified because the service bureau can't meet their turnaround requirements or because they have qualms about letting confidential data leave the organization.

CAR

Not only do computers serve as a source of microfilm, but they can also be used to help retrieve information from microfilm. Hence, we have a second acronym—CAR (computer-assisted retrieval).

CAR combines the strengths of the computer with the advantages of microfilm. The computer has the ability to classify and retrieve information quickly in a variety of ways. However, computer storage has always been expensive, while microfilm has the capability of storing large amounts of data cheaply in a minimum of space. CAR merges the two systems. Thus, the computer is used to index data and search for it, while microfilm is used to store and display the information.

The variety of CAR systems is virtually limitless. Hence, it is impossible to describe a typical CAR system. However, the basic principle is that when a document enters the system and is filmed, it is encoded and indexed by the computer. Because the computer indexes the material, filming can be done randomly. When retrieval is desired, the user requests the particular document or type of information, and the computer locates it.

CAR can be used with all types of microforms, although most roll-film systems use 16-mm cartridges. Microfiche and aperture cards are also popular choices. CAR can be used for both source-document microfilm and COM. With a COM system, the index can be prepared either at the same time the text is generated or after it is outputted to COM.

Like COM, CAR can be either on-line or off-line. If the system is off-line, the computer provides the data's location on the film. The operator then retrieves the film and advances it to the appropriate location using an off-line reader. If the system is on-line, the computer—through an interface with a micrographics terminal—can also advance the film to the appropriate location.

CAR is still a relatively new area in micrographics. However, the selection of micrographics terminals (combination reader-printer/terminals) is growing, and the newer terminals are able to inferface with a wider range of computers. Some experts anticipate that CAR will become the largest growth area in micrographics.

WHERE TO BEGIN

Now that you're familiar with the various types of microforms, equipment, and applications, it's time to consider designing a system. The problem here is that all too many organizations don't design a system first. Instead, they meet with vendors, review and select equipment, and then design a system. The result is frequently a disaster—not because the equipment is inferior, but because it is not the right equipment for that company's needs. Only after the system is planned and the needs determined should the equipment be selected.

Key Considerations

Developing a micrographics system involves a number of considerations. Only after you've determined your needs in these areas will you have the data necessary to design a system that's right for your company. These areas of consideration include:

1. *The physical characteristics of the records to be filmed.* For example, what are they—engineering drawings, checks, 8½″ × 11″ single sheets, or bound books? In addition to the records' physical nature,

you'll need to consider their size, the weight of the paper, their color, and whether both sides need to be filmed. As you'll recall, all of these factors will affect your choice of equipment.

Also, don't forget the overall quality of the documents. If it's very poor, you may not be able to get a satisfactory film copy. And if the paper is brittle or very fragile, it won't be able to pass through a rotary camera.

2. *The records' retention period.* You shouldn't begin your micro-filming program until the retention period is established, because it's pointless to film records that should be thrown away. Likewise, if the records have a low retention period and infrequent referrals, filming may not be cost-effective.

While you'll have to calculate the relative costs for your organiza-tion, a rough rule of thumb is that it's usually worthwhile to film if the records will be kept at least eight to ten years. If the records are actively referenced or needed in the office area for most of their life, filming may be justified with a lower retention period. Also, if the records are vital, filming duplicate copies for off-site storage is cheaper than making and storing duplicate paper copies.

When converting to microfilm, start filming current records as they're created rather than the backlog. If you begin with the backlog, you may never catch up to the present. Also, you'll realize the system's greatest benefits by converting present records to film and being able to take advantage of the greater productivity a film system offers during the records' period of most active use.

3. *The volume of records generated.* The system must be capable of filming the records as they're created, without long backlogs.

4. *The update frequency of the records.* If the records are to be updated, your primary options are a microjacket system, updatable microfiche, and COM. If the records must be updated more frequently than once every 24 hours, you had better consider an on-line system instead of microfilm.

5. *The access frequency of the records.* Be sure to consider how frequently the records are retrieved, how many people handle retrieval, and how quickly the records must be retrieved. One of the great advantages of microfilm is that it speeds retrieval and also makes it possible for large active files to be kept in the office area at the users' fingertips. Also, if the records are frequently accessed, you'll want to consider either a cartridge system or one of the

unitized microforms, as these will be easiest for the users to work with.

6. *The number of copies desired.* As a rule, unitized microforms are easier and cheaper to duplicate than the various roll-film applications. By having users work with film copies, such as duplicate fiche, the integrity of the master file can be protected.

7. *The hard-copy requirements.* As mentioned earlier, if hard copies of the records are needed extensively, microfilm may not be a good option. In any case, you'll need to determine how frequently hard copies will be *needed* and how many reader-printers will be required. Do keep the number of reader-printers to a minimum. You can add more later if necessary, but you do want users to become comfortable with film and not depend on a paper crutch.

8. *Organizing and indexing the records.* You also need to consider the best way of organizing the data—for example, one customer per fiche or the sequential order of documents on roll film. Roll film can be encoded in a variety of ways to speed retrieval, while fiche and jackets work well for unit files. CAR increases your options even more, as it permits random filming with the computer doing the indexing.

9. *Turnaround criteria.* You should also consider how quickly documents need to be converted to usable film. This factor can determine whether you film in-house or use a service bureau and, with an in-house system, the type of camera and processor you need.

10. *The future needs.* When planning a micrographics system, you should consider not only your present requirements but also future growth and applications. For example, if you plan to do source-document microfiche at 24X and go into COM fiche later at 48X, it makes sense to acquire readers now that can handle both reduction levels.

Three major considerations remain: the legality of microfilm, the decision of whether to go in-house or use a service bureau, and quality control. Each of these areas merits a separate discussion.

LEGALITY OF MICROFILM

When designing a system, you need to make sure the filmed records will be legally accepted by those government and regulatory bodies you deal with. In addition to verifying that the appropriate groups will accept film, you need to make sure your system meets any special conditions or requirements these groups have established for film systems.

As we've already noted, microforms are generally accepted by most states and the federal government as copies admissible in evidence in courts of law. The primary basis is statutory, under the Uniform Photographic Copies of Business and Public Records as Evidence Act (UPA). The federal version of the UPA is Title 28, Section 1732 of the U.S. Code for the Federal Government. Forty-four states have also adopted the UPA or legislation substantially equivalent to it.

The UPA sets four conditions that must be met before a copy can be admissible:

1. The record must be made in the ordinary course of business.

2. The copy must be made in the regular course of business. This can be demonstrated by preparing a declaration of intent and purpose similar to Figure 18. This statement should:

Identify the records and the company they belong to.
Identify the person who authorized the filming.
State the date the policy began.
State if the original will be destroyed.

The statement can be either filmed on each roll or simply kept separately on paper (an easier practice when fiche is involved).

3. The process used must accurately reproduce or form a durable medium for reproducing the original.

4. The copy must be satisfactorily identified. Normally, this identification is accomplished by a certificate of authenticity that:

Describes the first and last images on the film.
States which business owns the records and who filmed them.
Gives the date and location of the filming.

Figure 19 is an example of such a statement and can be either filmed (especially in the case of roll film) or kept separately.

In addition to the UPA, there is a basis for legal acceptance of microfilm under the Federal Rules of Evidence (Title 29, Section 2075 of the U.S. Code) and the 1953 and 1974 versions of the Uniform Rules of Evidence (which 11 states have adopted). Com-

Figure 18. Declaration of intent and purpose.

I, _____, employed by _____,
          name, title   company

do hereby declare that the _____ microfilmed herein
                                name of records

are the actual records of _____ created during its
                            company

normal course of business, and that:

It is the express intent and purpose of this organization to destroy or otherwise dispose of the original records microphotographed herein, and that:

The destruction or disposition of the records microphotographed is only to be accomplished after the inspection of the microfilm to assure completeness of coverage, and that·

From this day forward, it is the policy of this organization to microfilm and dispose of these original records as part of the planned organizational operating procedure.

Date _____Signature _____

Place _____Title _____
       city   state
                             Company _____

Figure 19. Certificate of authenticity.

This is to certify that the microphotographs appearing on this reel (or these microforms), starting with _____ and ending with _____, are accurate and complete reproductions of the records of _____, as
                                     company, department

delivered in the regular course of business for photographing.

Date produced _____Camera operator _____

City _____State _____

mon law also provides some basis for the acceptance of microfilm copies. And a variety of statutes deal with the microfilming of specific documents or types of evidence.

Although the vast majority of statutes permit filming, there are exceptions on both the state and federal levels. These include a number of rulings by federal regulatory agencies. The best source of current information in this area is *Legality of Microfilm,* Robert F. Williams, editor (Chicago: Cohasset Associates, Inc., 1980).

IN-HOUSE OR SERVICE BUREAU?

One final decision related to using micrographics is whether to film in-house or have a service bureau handle your filming. Of course, a large part of the decision is financial. You'll need to determine whether, for the volume of work you have, a service bureau or in-house will be cheaper. Another key consideration is turnaround time. If a service bureau cannot meet your needs in this area, you will be forced to go in-house.

Even if in-house is cheaper, you might want to begin with a service bureau and gradually go in-house as you develop a system and train personnel. Or you might want to consider a third option—filming in-house but having your film processed outside. This would free you from worries about the quality control aspects of film processing.

Another possibility is using a service bureau for specialty work where your volume does not justify in-house filming. For example, you might have adequate work for a rotary camera but not enough oversize drawings to justify a large planetary model. In that instance, a service bureau could be used for the drawings. Service bureaus can also be used for backlogs and, of course, for COM.

If you do use a service bureau, you'll probably still find it cheaper to prepare documents for filming in-house. By preparing documents, we mean removing staples and paper clips, taping tears, purging duplicates, and so forth. Document preparation is labor-intensive, and most service bureaus cannot perform it as cheaply as you can in-house.

Even if you plan to do your filming in-house, it's still a good idea to investigate service bureaus in your area. First of all, you can learn a great deal about microfilming by visiting service bureaus. After all, they earn their living by filming; they're experts. So observe their procedures and choice of equipment. Also, although you don't plan to use a service bureau now, you may unexpectedly have a need for one later. If you're already familiar with the bureaus in your area, making a decision will be much easier.

QUALITY CONTROL

Micrographics is a highly technical area. And as in many technical fields, quality control is an essential consideration. If you're using a service bureau or outside processor, it should perform these checks for you. If you're filming in-house, the responsibility is yours.

There are four basic aspects to quality control:

Residual thiosulfate
Resolution
Density
Film inspection and legibility

Residual thiosulfate. If you've ever developed film, you're probably familiar with the term "hypo." "Hypo," or thiosulfate, is the chemical commonly used in the developing process to "fix" film. If too much thiosulfate remains on the film after it is developed, the thiosulfate will eventually cause the film to deteriorate. Therefore, a chemical test—normally methylene blue—must be used to check the residue level. ANSI (the American National Standards Institute, 1430 Broadway, New York, N.Y. 10015) gives standards and procedures for measuring residual thiosulfate in Standard PH4.8. Note that this test only applies to wet processed silver film, as thiosulfate is not used in developing other types of microfilm.

Resolution. The second quality control area—resolution— measures the micrographic system's capability to separate fine detail. A chart like Figure 20 is filmed, and the patterns are examined under a microscope to determine the smallest pattern in which lines can be distinguished both horizontally and vertically. The appropriate standard is ANSI/ISO 3374-1979. Resolution tests are not normally applied to COM production, because alphanu-

Figure 20. The National Bureau of Standards resolution test chart.

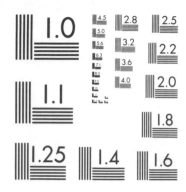

meric business COM recorders cannot generate the line patterns that make up the resolution test chart.

Density. Density is the opacity or the degree of darkness of the "black" portion of the film—the background on negative film. Density is measured by a special piece of equipment called a densitometer. For source-document negative microfilm, the reading should range from .9 to 1.3, depending on the type of original. For negative film COM, the density should be above 1.5.

Film inspection and legibility. Our last major quality control area is the simplest yet the most important. It requires no chemical tests or elaborate equipment, just a reader. Film inspection and legibility means just that: visually inspecting each image of the film to check that it is properly positioned and legible. This should *always* be done before the originals are destroyed.

Admittedly, this sounds like a simple, obvious precaution. Yet perhaps because it is so obvious, it is sometimes neglected—with disastrous results. For example, a few years ago, when two major stock brokerage firms merged, large masses of documents were quickly filmed by temporary workers and then destroyed.

It was subsequently discovered that one temporary had filmed documents for three days with no film in the camera. One might imagine the firms' customers were not too pleased when they read the story on the front page of *The Wall Street Journal.* A simple quality control check would have prevented the problem.

One other quality control item—if drawings to scale are being filmed and will later be restored to their original size, checking the reduction scale of the camera is important.

As you can see, micrographics is a highly technical area. To cover it in depth would require a book at least this size. Thus, this chapter must serve as an overview. A number of technical reference works are cited in the Bibliography. The National Micrographics Association is also an excellent source for more information.

CHAPTER 11

Documenting the Records Management Program

Up to now, we've been discussing how to develop an effective records management system and supporting procedures. However, having a well-designed system is not enough. You must also communicate the system both to its users and to those who will help you implement it. The records manual will be your communications vehicle.

THE MANUAL'S AUDIENCE

Before we can discuss the contents of such a manual or the way to prepare it, we must identify the manual's users. Typically, they fall into three main categories.

The first group is the individuals who will be responsible for implementing the program in their respective departments. This group normally includes the departmental records coordinators and the department heads. These individuals need two types of information: (1) an overall understanding of the program and their responsibilities within it, and (2) the practical information necessary to implement the program on an ongoing basis.

Our second group is the staff of the records management department. In addition to the information needed by the first group, they must also have detailed procedures for the internal operations of the records management program. For example, the first group only needs to know how to send records to the records center and request their retrieval. However, the second group must know exactly how to index the records and how to retrieve them and record that fact.

The third group includes the general users of the program—anyone who might need a record—in other words, practically everyone else in the company. These individuals need to know such general information as how to request a record from the records center or central files and how to use a microfilm reader.

Now the obvious question is how to meet all of these special interests without either overwhelming everyone with a monster manual that documents all details of the programs or writing three unique manuals. The answer is a modularized system of records manuals.

The large number of general users will receive a brief booklet that provides the practical information they need to use the system. The department heads and departmental records coordinators will receive a basic "core" manual. In addition to the information for general users, the core manual contains the policies and procedures needed to implement the program within the departments. The records department's manual includes the core plus the internal working procedures of the system. Thus, one documentation process serves all three groups.

With this approach, you'll probably find it easier to prepare the core material first and then expand upon it for the records management staff and reduce it for the general users. You may also want to print the additional material for the records management staff on colored paper so as to clearly differentiate it from the rest of the manual.

ISSUING THE MANUAL IN SECTIONS

As we've already discussed, the records management program must be developed gradually. Consequently, it is appropriate that the manual be developed in conjunction with the system, instead of after the entire program is operational.

If you follow this approach, the sectional order of the records manual will depend on how your program has evolved. For example, if your program has begun with records retention, the first three sections of the manual to be issued will be:

1. Program Overview
2. Records Retention
3. Records Center

Program Overview

The overview section states the program's goals and the responsibilities of key personnel. These personnel include the records manager, the department heads, the departmental records coordinators, and any supervisors reporting to the records manager. This last group might include the micrographics supervisor, the records center supervisor, and the central files supervisor, assuming, of course, that you don't wear all of these hats as part of your job. With the exception of the department heads, the statements of responsibility can be condensed from the job descriptions for the various positions.

The department heads' responsibilities are:

1. To insure that the records management program is fully implemented in their areas, in accordance with the guidelines specified by the records management staff.
2. To appoint records coordinators for their areas.
3. To insure that these coordinators have the time and resources needed to perform their job.

Spelling all this out may seem like you're belaboring an obvious point. But the department heads' support is essential to the program's success.

This initial section of the manual should emphasize the fact that the records management program is an ongoing effort, not a one-time endeavor. It should also state whatever audits or follow-ups will be conducted to insure the program's success. This section is basically the same for all three versions of the manual, although you might want to condense it for the general users' booklet.

Records Retention

The records retention or disposition section of the manual begins with a statement of the organization's overall retention/disposition policy. Typically, such a policy states that the organization retains records only as long as they are needed for administrative and archival purposes or required by legal and regulatory groups. The policy also requires all departments to comply with the established retention periods and specifies that these periods will be reviewed annually.

Next is a statement of the procedures for setting and reviewing retention periods. These procedures should include an explanation of administrative, fiscal, legal, and archival values. The remainder of the section is the records retention schedule, which should be displayed on a form similar to that in Figure 3 (Chapter 4).

This section of the manual is the same for both the core version and the records management staff's version. The general users' guide should state the overall retention policy, emphasizing the importance of destroying records only in accordance with the schedule. This guide refers users to the core manual or to their records coordinators for specific retention values.

Records Center

The core version of this section states the center's purpose (storage of inactive records in accordance with the official retention policy). It also gives the procedures for transferring records to the center, requesting records from the center, and destroying records at the end of their retention period.

In addition to the core material, the records management staff's section includes the procedures for:

Indexing records and assigning box numbers.
Locating and retrieving records.
Maintaining the tickler file.
Handling and releasing confidential records.
Issuing and maintaining the automated index, if any.
Preparing center activity and accuracy reports.

It should also include fire, safety, and security procedures and any other information necessary for the proper internal operation of the center.

The users' guide briefly states the center's purpose, explaining that records are sent over at the end of their active use period and destroyed according to the schedule. It also includes the procedure for requesting records from the center—a concern to most users.

Vital Records

When the vital records program is developed, it should be documented in the manual in a separate section. The core section for this topic includes:

The company's official definition of a vital record.

The procedure for determining if a record is vital, including a definition of the vital records committee's role in the process.

The procedure for sending records off-site to the vital records center and retrieving them.

If you'll be testing the program's effectiveness periodically, you'll also want to give guidelines for the tests. The remainder of the section will be devoted to the vital records schedule, which should be printed on a form similar to Figure 8 (Chapter 6).

Normally, the core version of the section will also suffice for the records management staff. However, if the company maintains its own internal vital records center, procedures for its operation must be given. The users' guide need only give the definition of a vital record and refer users to the core manual or their records coordinator for more information.

Filing

This section's contents depend on the type of controls you have for the filing of active records. If there is a central files program, you'll need to give procedures for sending records to central files, retrieving them, and returning them. These procedures would appear in all three versions of the manual. The manual for the records management staff would also include the procedures for operating the central files room.

If there is also a uniform filing system, all three manuals should state the various classifications in the system, their definitions, and an index to the system. If the uniform system is used on a decentralized basis instead of in a central files room, the core manual would explain how to implement the system on a departmental basis.

On the other hand, if each department maintains its own files without the benefit of a uniform filing system, you'll want to give some general guidelines for files maintenance. These might include requiring the use of ARMA's alphabetic filing rules and describing the various types of filing systems, such as terminal-digit, along with suggested applications for each.

If files audits will be conducted, this section of the core manual should state the procedures that will be followed, the standards that must be met, and the follow-up for departments not in compliance. The core manual should also state the company's policy on purchasing filing equipment. A key part of this policy is the requirement that the records manager must approve all requests for new filing equipment and that requests will be approved only if the department is in compliance with the retention schedule.

Forms and Reports Management

The three manuals' sections on forms and reports management will be quite similar. Once again, this material will be added to the manuals as the programs go into effect.

Each section in all three manuals will begin with an official policy statement that forms (or reports) can be created only with the knowledge and the authorization of the records management staff. The three manuals will also define forms and reports and include the procedures for:

Requesting new forms or reports.
Requesting changes in existing forms and reports.
Discontinuing existing forms and reports.

In addition to this material, the records management staff's manual will include all the internal working procedures in both areas. Examples would be procedures for:

Establishing and maintaining the functional files.
Assigning form and report numbers.
Reordering forms.
Maintaining the forms inventory control system.

Micrographics

If micrographics is widely used in the organization, you may want to include in the three manuals procedures for the proper use of readers, reader-printers, and film. Of course, the records management staff manual would also include detailed operational procedures, quality standards, and so forth.

Other Sections

The sections just discussed are the ones most likely to appear in a records manual. Another possible section might give detailed procedures for the use, dissemination, and destruction of confidential records. This material is most likely to be required in manuals for organizations where security is a prime concern, such as a government defense contractor. Some organizations also include a special section on the legal aspects of corporate records. This is done when legal considerations are a key factor for the company.

PREPARING THE MANUAL

Whatever the topics you choose to include in the records manual, the preparation process remains basically the same. Also, preparing a records manual is simpler than preparing other types of administrative manuals. That's because you do not have to go to other departments to collect the data for the manual; you are the source of the data, as well as the manual's preparer. And there is less text to write for a records manual because the retention and vital records schedules comprise a large portion of the manual.

Where to Begin

A logical starting point is to develop a comprehensive working outline for the three manuals. The outlines should include each section title and the specific topics to be discussed in that section. For example:

II. Records Retention
    A. Overall policy
    B. Procedure for setting retention periods
    C. Procedure for reviewing the retention schedule
    D. Retention schedule

After you've prepared the outlines, get them approved by the same people who must review and approve the entire manual. Then if there are any differences of opinion as to a manual's overall content, you'll be able to resolve them before you begin writing.

The Manual's Physical Appearance

The next step is to plan the manual's physical appearance. Although you will sometimes see records manuals prepared as bound booklets, this is not advisable because updating the manual will be virtually impossible. A three-ring binder is a more long-lasting and practical approach, though initially more expensive. The only exception is the users' guide, which changes less frequently and may therefore be done as a booklet.

Order a binder large enough that additional material can be added later. If you're beginning with the overview, retention, and records center sections, you'll probably want to start with the binder half full.

While the binder's design is up to your creativity, it's a good idea to select a dark color that will not show dirt easily. Also, the manual should be clearly identified on its spine so the users can distinguish it from other corporate manuals on the bookshelf. If you're on a tight budget or are distributing only a few manuals, you may want to purchase stock binders with metal or plastic pockets on the spine for identification cards.

Another option is binders with clear vinyl pockets on the front, back, and spine. Inserts identifying the manual are printed on card stock and inserted into the pockets. This approach allows the organization to bulk-order binders and use them for a variety of purposes. But do avoid binders with pockets on the inside covers; users have a regrettable tendency to "file" updates to the manual in these pockets.

For easy referencing, each section of the manual should be identified with an index tab. The tabs should be Mylar-reinforced and should state both the section number and title ("02 Records Retention," for example). The holes on the tab sheets should also be Mylar-reinforced.

Page Headings

Each page of the manual (except the schedules) should have a standard page heading that clearly identifies it as part of the records manual. Then if the page is removed from the manual, it can easily be replaced in the proper position. The reason we exempted the schedules from this requirement is that the forms given in Chapters 4 and 6 provide the necessary information and make a further heading repetitious.

If your company has other manuals with standard page headings, you can model yours on those. Or you can develop a simple page design similar to Figure 21.

RECORDS MANUAL

Logo

Subject:

Number:

Page:

Date:

Figure 21. Records manual sample page design.

The subject refers to the specific topic, such as "Transferring Records to the Records Center." The number is usually a two-part reference to the section and specific topic. For example, 02-03 is the third topic in the second section. Each subject is also page-numbered separately, beginning with page 1. Then if we expand 02-03 from two pages to four, the pages in 02-04, 02-05, and so on will not have to be renumbered.

It is a good idea to place "Cont." at the bottom of each page and "End" at the bottom of the last page. Otherwise a user might be missing a page and not realize it. Another approach is to use "page 1 of 4," "page 2 of 4," and so on. However, with this method the entire section must be reprinted if it is lengthened or shortened.

Each page should also have the date that page was issued. When the page is revised, the date is changed accordingly. Then it's a simple matter for the users to compare the dates and determine which page is current practice.

Introductory Material

A records manual should have a table of contents; that is, a listing of sections and topics in the order in which they may occur. The table of contents serves as the users' reference guide to the entire manual. Figure 22 is a sample portion of a records manual's table of contents.

Unlike other manuals, a records manual does not normally need an index. That's because the table of contents is self-explanatory and relatively short, and because the retention and vital records schedules form their own index through alphabetic listings.

However, you should include a brief introduction that explains:

The manual's purpose
Who should use it
Who approved it
How to use it

The "how to use it" material in the introduction will include an explanation of the manual's overall organization and numbering system. It will also state the users' responsibilities concerning the manual. These include:

Following the manual's policies and procedures.
Keeping their copies up to date.

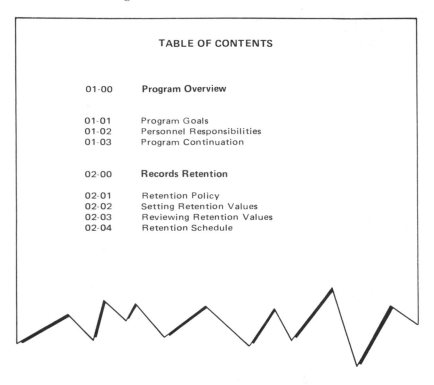

Figure 22. Sample table of contents.

Turning their copies in when they leave the organization.
Notifying the records manager of any changes or revisions, such
as new records series.

Writing Clearly and Concisely

If the manual is to be a success, the text must be written clearly
and concisely. The records manual is not the place for pompous,
lengthy sentences extolling the virtues of the records program. Two
simple rules will help you avoid that problem:

Write in the active voice.
Eliminate deadwood.

Writing in the active voice means that the subject of the sentence
performs the action. For example:

List each carton separately on the transfer list. ("You" is the subject and is understood.)

OR

The central files supervisor completes the report daily. ("The supervisor" is the subject.)

The active voice is concise, and it always assigns responsibility—a must in a manual. The difference becomes obvious if you rewrite the examples above in the passive voice, with the subject being acted upon.

Each carton should be listed separately on the transfer list.

OR

The report is completed daily. ("By the central files supervisor" may be added.)

The other key to good writing is eliminating "deadwood," or unnecessary words. Make sure every word is there for a reason. For example, why say "in the event that" or "due to the fact that" when "if" and "because" will do the job much better? Also avoid repetitious phrases such as "plan in advance" and "basic essentials."

If you feel unsure of your writing skills or would like a quick brushup, read *The Elements of Style* by William Strunk, Jr., and E. B. White (third edition, Macmillan, 1979). In slightly over 90 pages, Strunk and White say everything you need to know about good writing.

Playscript Procedures

Much of the writing you'll be doing in the manual is procedural— "how to do something." Typical procedures might be: "Requesting a Record from the Records Center," "Transferring Records to the Records Center," and "Requesting a New Form."

Since most of these procedures involve more than one person, you'll find it helpful to write them in "playscript."* In other words, write the procedure as if it were the script for a play. The only difference is that the "actors" perform specific tasks in the proce-

*Playscript was developed by Leslie Matthies and is discussed in his book *The New Playscript Procedure* (Stamford, Conn.: Office Publications, Inc., 1977).

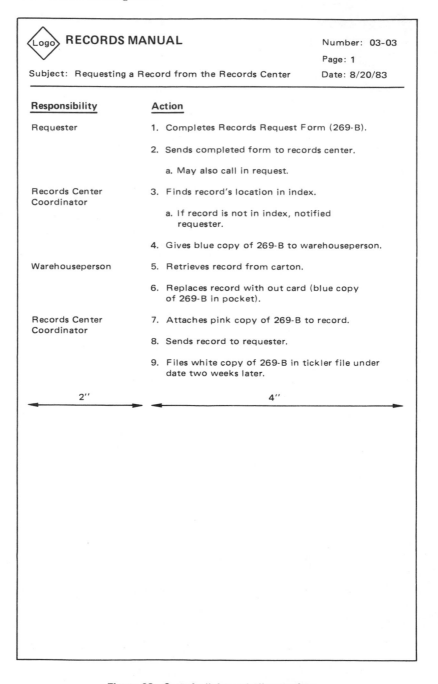

◇ Logo ◇ **RECORDS MANUAL**   Number: 03-03

Page: 1

Subject: Requesting a Record from the Records Center   Date: 8/20/83

Responsibility	Action
Requester	1. Completes Records Request Form (269-B).
	2. Sends completed form to records center.
	a. May also call in request.
Records Center Coordinator	3. Finds record's location in index.
	a. If record is not in index, notified requester.
	4. Gives blue copy of 269-B to warehouseperson.
Warehouseperson	5. Retrieves record from carton.
	6. Replaces record with out card (blue copy of 269-B in pocket).
Records Center Coordinator	7. Attaches pink copy of 269-B to record.
	8. Sends record to requester.
	9. Files white copy of 269-B in tickler file under date two weeks later.

←———— 2″ ————→   ←———————— 4″ ————————→

Figure 23. Sample "playscript" procedure.

dure instead of speaking lines of dialog. Figure 23 is an example of a playscript procedure.

As you can see, playscript forces you into a concise, logical writing style. It also makes it easy for each individual to identify his or her responsibilities. If an exception or other option occurs, it is broken out and listed separately, just as was done with 2a.

Do note the column proportions marked on Figure 23. Limiting the responsibilitiy column to two inches is necessary if you are to have an adequate line length for the actions.

Forms in the Manual

Any forms mentioned in the manual should be reproduced in it. This enables users to know what the form looks like and insures that they use the right form. For example, in the playscript procedure just presented, you'd include as an attachment a filled-in sample of Form 269-B. This attachment would be placed at the end of the procedure. Since a properly designed form is self-explanatory, you won't need to include instructions on how to complete the form.

GETTING THE MANUAL APPROVED

After the manual is written, you'll need to get it approved. Typically, this approval group will include senior executives—not because they care how you retrieve or transfer records but because they do care about the overall policies and disposition schedule.

In some cases, you may find executives hesitant to approve the manual because they feel unsure of their knowledge in this area. Several things will help speed the process. First, be sure the reviewers know who has already approved the material, such as the legal, fiscal, and administrative representatives, and how the decisions were made. Second, ask them to set their own deadline for reviewing the material. People are more likely to meet a deadline if they set it. Of course, you'll confirm the deadline in writing with a "thank-you" note.

Third, a few days before the material is due back, give the reviewers a "friendly reminder." That's a phone call to ask if they have any questions so far—much more tactful than "Have you looked at it yet?" This approach is usually effective. However, if you have further problems with an unusually recalcitrant reviewer, document all your efforts to get a response and then go to your boss for help.

PRODUCING THE MANUAL

If at all possible, the manual should be prepared on a word processing system. This will greatly simplify the process of preparing revised drafts, as well as making changes at a later date. Be sure to proofread the material carefully, especially the numbers in the schedules. An error there can be disastrous.

Normally, such a manual is reproduced from typed copy rather than typeset because of the limited number of copies and cost considerations. For the same reasons, the manual is generally printed in-house or even reproduced on a photocopier. Do be sure, however, that all forms and illustrations are clearly reproduced and legible.

DISTRIBUTING THE MANUAL

If at all possible, it's a good idea to give out the manual at a training session/kick-off meeting. This will give you an opportunity to review its contents carefully with the users and answer any questions they may have about the system. Likewise, when new sections to the manual are introduced, you'll find additional training sessions helpful.

KEEPING THE MANUAL UP TO DATE

Any manual quickly loses its effectiveness if it's not kept up to date. And as we've already discussed, the schedules should be reviewed annually to incorporate new records and reduce retention values. You should also review the remainder of the manual annually. This review will enable you to pick up those procedural changes that were not incorporated into the manual when they occurred. The review also allows you to reassess existing policies and determine if they are still appropriate.

Don't delegate this task. You'll be surprised at the changes you'll find—even when you think the manual is up to date. However, it's a good backup to have other staff members, such as the records center supervisor, review appropriate sections. They may catch corrections you've overlooked.

Updating the manual also involves making sure users keep their copies of the manual up to date. As a follow-up, it's a good idea to incorporate a spot check of the manuals into the files audit. If a manual has three of the last year's revisions, it's safe to assume that it's up to date. Otherwise, the entire manual should be checked and updated.

CHAPTER 12

The Legal Aspects of Records Management

In addition to the legal retention requirements we discussed in Chapter 4, a variety of other legislation affects records management. This legislation has been developed to meet two objectives. The first objective is to control the paperwork reporting burden the federal government places on itself and others. The second is to protect the individual's rights and privacy, primarily from intrusion by the government. Both goals are highly desirable; both have proved difficult to attain.

EARLY LEGISLATION

Our history of records management legislation begins with the Federal Reports Act of 1942. Until April 1981, this Act served as the government's primary means of controlling the paperwork burden it placed on citizens and others. As you've probably guessed, the Act was less than totally successful, especially in later years. As a result, it was superseded by the Paperwork Reduction Act of 1980.

The other early piece of records management legislation—the Federal Records Act of 1950—provided the legislative background for the federal records management program. The Act required each agency to provide an efficient, economical program for the management of its records. The agencies were to cooperate with the General Services Administration (GSA) in their records management efforts. Of course, "cooperate" is a rather loose term, and the paperwork continued to increase. The complaints from the private sector also increased.

Consequently, as part of the Privacy Act of 1974, Congress established the Commission on Federal Paperwork. The commission was in effect for two years (1975–1977) and made approximately 800 recommendations. The legislative process, however, moves slowly, and it was not until December 1980 that any major legislation relating to paperwork reduction was passed.

THE PAPERWORK REDUCTION ACT OF 1980

This legislation was the Paperwork Reduction Act of 1980 (PL 96-511). Its stated purposes were:

To reduce the paperwork burden the federal government places on others.

To minimize the cost to the government of gathering and using information, while increasing the information's usefulness.

To standardize as much as possible federal information policies and practices.

To improve the government's use of automated data processing and telecommunications technologies.

To insure that the government collects and uses information in compliance with the Privacy Act.

As a means of achieving these goals, the Act established the Office of Information and Regulatory Affairs as part of the Office of Management and Budget (OMB). This office's function is to review and approve federal agency rules, regulations, forms, and systems that place a paperwork burden on others. The agency's goal as expressed in the Act is to reduce the public's reporting burden by 25 percent over the next five years.

The Act also requires the Office of Information and Regulatory Affairs to establish the Federal Information Locator System (FILS). FILS will include an index reference to every data profile required by the federal government. It will not include the actual data collected but will serve as an authoritative register of all government information collection requests. Its purpose is to eliminate duplicate requests by different agencies. With this system, a company or individual should have to supply data only once to the federal government. If another agency needs the same information, it will collect it from the first agency rather than from the company. Collection, however, will be with the company's knowledge, and the public, as well as the government, will be able to access FILS.

In addition to the above records management areas, the Paperwork Reduction Act also specifies various improvements in the federal ADP (automated data processing) systems.

Of course, the key question is whether or not the Act will accomplish its goals. Although the Act was initially greeted with great enthusiasm, at present the outcome is questionable. One potential difficulty is that much of the paperwork government agencies require is in support of congressional statutes. And while the Act mandates reducing the paperwork burden, it does not control the statutes that require the paperwork.

Another apparent problem area is that, as of this writing, the Office of Information and Regulatory Affairs has moved slowly in implementing the Act. Consequently, the federal agencies are assuming a wait-and-see posture, maintaining that they need guidelines from the office before they can act.

One result of the current concern over the Paperwork Reduction Act's slow implementation has been proposed legislation to reduce federally mandated retention requirements. In its current form, such legislation would establish a four-year retention period for any federally required records except those required by the Internal Revenue Code of 1954 and those dealing with hazardous wastes and materials. If this or similar legislation is passed, it will greatly simplify the preparation of retention schedules, as well as substantially reduce the amount of records most organizations must keep.

PROTECTING THE INDIVIDUAL'S RIGHTS

As the federal government grew and gathered more information about the public, concern about the uses of that information, as well as about the reporting burden, grew also. That concern about the uses increased as data processing made it possible to access and compile that data in a variety of ways. Consequently, legislation was passed in an effort to control the government's use of information about the public.

The Freedom of Information Act

The first such piece of legislation was the Freedom of Information Act (FOIA), passed in 1966. This Act gave citizens the right of access to information government agencies collect and the records they maintain—unless the agencies can legally justify withholding the information.

In 1974, the Freedom of Information Act was amended to increase the government agencies' accountability. These post-Watergate amendments required publication of an index to documents collected and maintained by the government. The amendments also require agencies to answer requests for information in 10 days and to respond to appeals in 20 days.

In recent years, the Act has come under attack for several reasons. Many businesses feel that the Act provides insufficient protection against the disclosure of trade secrets and other confidential information to their competitors. Currently, the government can release data without notifying the company that submitted it of its release.

Several bills are before Congress now to correct that situation. The proposed legislation requires agencies to notify companies whenever there is a request for information they've submitted, as well as limits the types of information the agencies can disclose.

Another aspect of the Freedom of Information Act that has excited considerable controversy concerns law enforcement information. The argument is that information available through the Act can jeopardize the success of law enforcement operations. Consequently, proposals have been made to limit the amount of information the FBI and CIA must provide under the Act.

Another possible change to the Act would lengthen the time an agency has to respond to a request—unless that request is from the news media or for the public benefit. Many agency FOIA officers feel ten days is too short a response time, especially since the public often addresses the request incorrectly. Thus, several days may elapse before the request reaches the officer and can be evaluated. Proposals are also before Congress to increase the fees agencies will charge for responding to FOIA requests.

While it's impossible to predict what changes will be made, it does seem safe to assume that the Act will be modified in some ways in the near future.

The Privacy Act

The Privacy Act of 1974 was the other significant piece of post-Watergate legislation designed to protect the rights of the individual. This Act stated that individuals must have access to the records the government maintains about them. It also specifies that there should be no unforeseen use of the information that individuals supply unless they consent to it. Moreover, the information collected about individuals should, in most circumstances, be collected directly from them, should be collected only when necessary, and must be accurate. The individual also has the right to exclude others from certain federal agency records. In other words, the Act protects the individual's privacy from intrusions due to the Freedom of Information Act.

The Privacy Act also established the Commission on Federal Paperwork, whose work we've already discussed, and the Privacy Protection Study Commission. This second group studied privacy in both the public and private sectors. It was in effect for two years and made a variety of recommendations both for specific organizations, such as insurance companies and medical care institutions, and for business and government in general. However, no major legislation equivalent to the Paperwork Reduction Act of 1980 has resulted from its work. Some privacy legislation dealing with specific types of organizations has passed, and some states have established their own privacy legislation.

Protecting Employee Privacy

Fortunately, many corporations have not waited for federal legislation on privacy in the private sector. They have gone ahead and established their own employee privacy protection programs. If your organization has not done so, now would be an excellent time to begin. Typically, such programs are developed through a combined effort by the records manager and the personnel department. After its creation, the program is usually maintained by the personnel department.

While privacy protection programs vary from organization to organization, the following features are fairly standard:

1. Employees have the right to see information the organization maintains about them. In particular, this includes their own personnel file. Certain information, such as future salary and promotion

plans, may be excluded. Employees also have the right to correct erroneous information in the file and dispute material with which they do not agree.

In fact, many companies that do not have full-blown privacy programs have set this policy. In some states, companies are even required by law to allow employees to see their personnel files.

2. As a corollary, the organization should collect personal information about the employee only when it has a valid reason. Equal Employment Opportunity legislation has done much already to help in this area, especially where hiring is concerned. Also, information about the employee should be collected only with the employee's knowledge and consent.

3. Managers should see only job-related information about their employees. For example, a manager should not see health or benefit information about the employee. The only exception would be a work-related need, such as the possibility of having to administer emergency medication or other first aid on the job, as a result of a specific physical condition.

4. Personal information on the employee should be retained only as long as necessary. For example, one major corporation keeps performance appraisals only three years. The rationale is that an employee should be judged only on recent performance. If the employee has improved, previous problems should not be allowed to prejudice a manager who might otherwise be unaware of them. And if the employee has not improved, the organization should have been able to resolve the situation in three years.

5. The organization should release only very limited information about the employee without the employee's written consent. For example, the only information one company releases without the employee's written consent is job title, place of work, and date of employment. Also, government agencies requesting other information about the employee may receive it only through the legal process—an important rule.

6. The organization should not maintain any secret personal information systems about its employees. Now, you may think, "That's so obvious; why have a rule about it?" But there are organizations with such systems. One hospital keeps "anecdotal" files on its nurses. These files contain administrators' opinions about the nurses and are not seen by the nurses. In fact, the nurses

are not even supposed to know the file exists. And in at least one case, totally inaccurate information was included in a nurse's file solely because the administrator did not like her and wished to hurt her career advancement.

7. Finally, the organization should document its privacy program and establish internal procedures to protect the security of such information. Managers should be trained in the privacy program and should be disciplined for any violations of an employee's privacy.

THE FUTURE

It's difficult to make predictions about possible new privacy legislation or other records management areas. However, you should keep abreast in these areas, as they are changing rapidly. ARMA does an excellent job of keeping its members posted on legislative developments, as well as lobbying for legislation that will benefit the records management profession.

Likewise, the entire field of records management is both changing and growing. You as a records manager must be able to change and adapt accordingly without losing sight of the basic objectives listed in Chapter 1. This book provides you with all the tools for a comprehensive, growing records management program—the rest is up to you. Good luck!

Bibliography

Association of Records Managers and Administrators, Inc., *Readings in Records Management*, Private Village, Kan.: ARMA, Inc., 1978.
———, *Readings in Records Management from the Records Management Quarterly, Volume II, October 1977–July 1980*. Prairie Village, Kan.: ARMA, Inc., 1980.
———, *Records Management Workshop*. Prairie Village, Kan.: ARMA, Inc., 1976.
———, *Rules for Alphabetical Filing*. Prairie Village, Kan.: ARMA, Inc., 1972.
Bankers Box/Records Storage Systems, *Records Control and Storage Handbook*. Itasca, Ill.: Bankers Box/Records Storage Systems, 1977.
Diamond, Susan Z., *How to Manage Administrative Operations*. New York: AMA Extension Institute, 1981.
———, *Preparing Administrative Manuals*. New York: AMACOM, 1981.
Fedders, John M., and Guttenplan, Lauryn H., "Document Retention and Destruction: Practical, Legal and Ethical Considerations." Reprinted from *The Notre Dame Lawyer (October 1980): 5–64*.
Federal Register, Guide to Record·Retention Requirements, 1981. Washington, D.C.: Office of the Federal Register, National Archives and Records Service, General Services Administration, 1981. (Note: This guide is published annually.)
Freedman, Alan, *The Computer Glossary*. New York: The Computer Language Company, Inc., 1981.
Journal of Micrographics. Silver Spring, Md.: National Micrographics Association. (Note: All issues will be of interest.)
Lybarger, Phyllis M., *Records Retention Scheduling*. Prairie Village, Kan.: ARMA, Inc., 1980.
Maedke, Dr. Wilmer, *Records Management Profession: Status and Trends* (ARMA Research Study No. 7). Prairie Village, Kan.: ARMA, Inc., 1976.
Mezher, Graham C., and Turner, Jeffery H., eds., *Micrographic Film Technology*. Silver Spring, Md.: National Micrographics Association, 1979.

National Micrographics Association, *An Introduction to Computer Output Microfilm*. Silver Spring, Md.: National Micrographics Association, 1980.

———, *An Introduction to Microform Indexing and Retrieval Systems*. Silver Spring, Md.: National Micrographics Association, 1980.

———, *An Introduction to Micrographics*. Silver Spring, Md.: National Micrographics Association, 1980.

———, *NMA Standard Practice for Operational Procedures/Inspection and Quality Control of First Generation Silver Gelatin Microfilm Documents* (MS23-1979). Silver Spring, Md.: National Micrographics Association, 1979.

Nygren, William V., *Business Forms Management*. New York: AMACOM, 1980.

Records Management Quarterly. Prairie Village, Kan.: ARMA, Inc. (Note: All issues will be of interest.)

Shelly, Gary B., and Cashman, Thomas J., *Introduction to Computers and Data Processing*. Fullerton, Calif.: Anaheim Publishing Company, 1980.

Williams, Robert F., ed., *Legality of Microfilm*. Chicago: Cohasset Associates, Inc., 1980.

Index